CHICAGO
Scavenger

Jessica Mlinaric

Copyright © 2022 by Reedy Press, LLC
Reedy Press
PO Box 5131
St. Louis, MO 63139, USA
www.reedypress.com

Library of Congress Control Number: 2021950830

ISBN: 9781681063584

Cover and interior design by Claire Ford

Cover and interior photos by Jessica Mlinaric

Clip art courtesy of Pixabay and Wikimedia Commons

Printed in the United States of America
22 23 24 25 26 5 4 3 2 1

Dedication

For Brett, my partner in exploring and all of life.

"The city is, I remind myself, an organic thing, ever-changing, remolding itself in the visions of developers and architects and politicians. And now perhaps the people will get in on the game."
—Rick Kogan

Contents

Acknowledgments

My wildest dream came true when *Secret Chicago: A Guide to the Weird, Wonderful, and Obscure* was published and I became an author. Thank you to the team at Reedy Press for that opportunity and for helping me bring a second book to life, especially Josh Stevens and Barbara Northcott. Molly Page, I can't thank you enough for that introduction!

Thanks to Hen Chung and Sarah Freeman for providing feedback and cheering me on throughout this project. To Blake Levinson and J. J. McDowell, the wine is on me next time.

Thank you to my *Secret Chicago* and urbnexplorer.com readers for sharing your stories and suggestions. The best part of writing a book is connecting with you.

To my family and friends, your encouragement means everything to me. Dad, thanks for always showing me that anything can be an adventure. Brett, thank you for your support in so many big and small ways. I couldn't have done this without you.

Introduction

"You've investigated speakeasies and buried nuclear debris. What's the most surprising thing you learned?" This was a common question after the publication of my book *Secret Chicago: A Guide to the Weird, Wonderful, and Obscure*. Yet, in a city where you can find intrigue and excitement around every corner, I was most surprised to learn how easy it is for Chicagoans to stay in their neighborhood bubble.

It all started in my grandma's backyard. My cousin and I spent hours drawing scavenger hunts and treasure maps to the patch of trees between her lawn and a neighboring grocery store parking lot. That little grove was a playground of magic and mystery, but Chicago, the city I moved to over a decade ago, was a treasure trove.

Invigorated by my new surroundings, I made it a personal mission to enjoy and learn about as much of Chicago as possible and share my findings. I started my blog, urbnexplorer.com, and expanded to freelance writing and photography for local and national publications.

In a city the size of Chicago, it can be hard to know where to begin exploring outside the usual routes around work and home. Speaking with readers and Chicago enthusiasts, I learned that they're curious about the city and crave fresh ways to experience it. I'm passionate about inspiring others to engage with people and places that are new to them, and see the familiar in a new light. *Chicago Scavenger* is your invitation to go out and do it!

Set forth on these scavenger hunts around 17 areas of Chicago. Some are contained within a neighborhood and some are community areas that span several neighborhoods. You can embark on these adventures in any order.

Each thrilling section includes a riddle and a photograph for 19 or more clues. Solving the clues will lead you to historic sites, public art, museums, restaurants, secret gardens, and more! The clues in every section are organized in a suggested route. Plan a day to complete each neighborhood. In addition to the public transit and parking information provided, I'd recommend biking, which is how I like to tour the city.

Whether you're cracking a clue on your own street (there's one on mine!) or visiting a neighborhood for the first time, I've tried to offer a feel for each area by choosing sites that are visually interesting, historically important, or meaningful to the cultural fabric of the neighborhood. It's challenging to convey this significance in just a few lines; I hope these clues spark your interest in learning more about the stories behind them.

Get ready for fun and surprises and join the hunt at chicagoscavenger.com! You can email here for a hint if you get stumped on a clue. Whether you're a devoted adventurer or you use this book for the occasional detour, you'll decode challenges to discover hidden gems while connecting with Chicago in a new way. Neighborhood by neighborhood, I hope you uncover Chicago's landmarks, community quirks, and local flavors, from the seemingly mundane to the magnificent. Let's embark!

CHICAGO

Legend

Rogers Park

Rogers Park is Chicago's northernmost community area. This lakefront location offers scenic views and under-the-radar beaches. As one of Chicago's most diverse neighborhoods, it features international dining and shopping and a colorful local arts scene. This hunt also visits the neighboring West Ridge community. Take the Red Line to Loyola station. Free and metered parking is available.

1

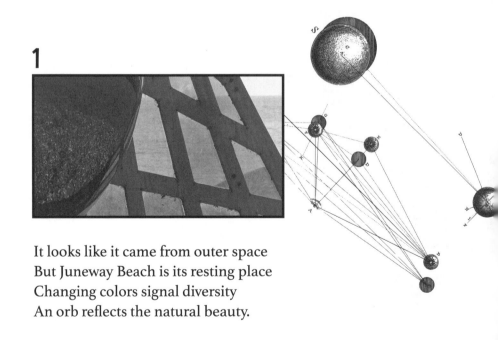

It looks like it came from outer space
But Juneway Beach is its resting place
Changing colors signal diversity
An orb reflects the natural beauty.

2

Look for a palm tree on the sign
That sweeps you off to island time
With tasty beef patties and jerk chicken
They guarantee you'll be finger lickin'.

_____

_____

3

Behind a city box, a sign
At Clark and Rogers recalls the line
Between indigenous and settler lands
A park bears its name, to the south it stands.

_____

_____

4

On Sheridan look for Prairie Style
You might decide to stay awhile
A Chicago home by Frank Lloyd Wright
You can even opt to spend the night.

_____

_____

5

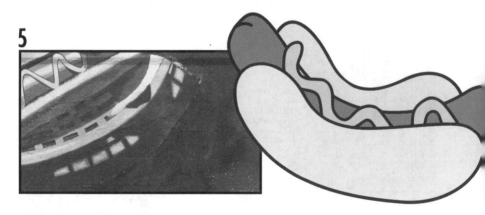

The Mile of Murals brightens the Red Line
One artwork, "Be Happy," is especially fine
A hot dog, abstracts, and much, much more
In the artist's nearby convenience store.

_____

_____

6

Once a former ComEd substation
Now showing literary adaptations
Here children's plays come alive
On stage since 1985.

7

Rogers Park's an artsy neighborhood
As you'll discover walking down Glenwood
One artist found objects some threw away
In this garden they're now transformed for display.

8

Near the lighthouse take a stroll
Wander down to the sandy knoll
Native landscape being restored
Admire the shorebirds and the forbs.

_____

_____

9

Along the lake for six hundred feet
You'll find Chicago's most colorful seat
It's refreshed in white every year
When neighbors paint it with good cheer.

_____

_____

10

'Twixt bland new buildings on Sheridan
A twenties terra-cotta gem still stands
Look up and trace Chicago's history
From Fort Dearborn to Blackstone and Wrigley.

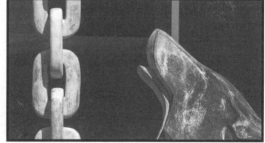

11

You can't miss two wolves eight feet tall
Where Loyola Ramblers play basketball
Praising the generosity
Of the whole Loyola family.

12

Our Lady built for the highway
Faces toward the lake today
The great rose window is divine
Ringed by four evangelist signs.

_____

_____

13

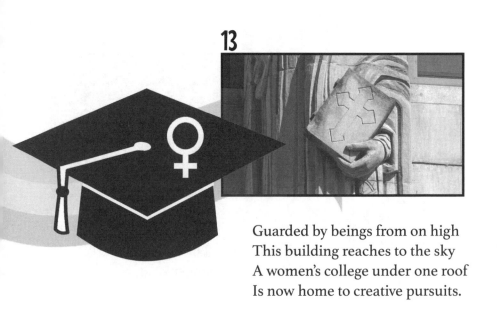

Guarded by beings from on high
This building reaches to the sky
A women's college under one roof
Is now home to creative pursuits.

_____

_____

14

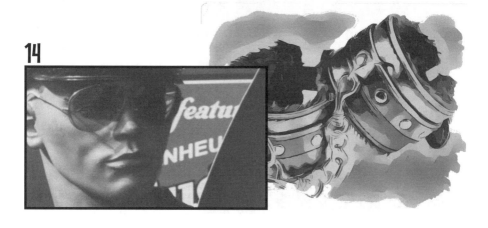

A simple brick building from the outside
Celebrates a subculture with pride
Displaying handcuffs, crops, and a dungeon
It is Chicago's raciest museum.

15

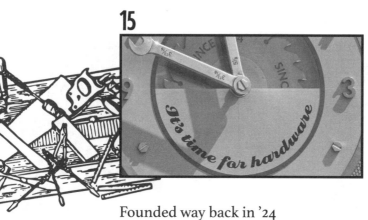

Founded way back in '24
The city's oldest hardware store
Owned by three generations of the same family
It's the source for all your home repair needs.

16

This library specializing in LGBTQ
Is open and accessible for anyone to view
Proud to preserve Midwest gay history
Advancing the cause of justice and equality.

_____

_____

17

When you are craving something sweet
Jalebi is just the right treat
Try every flavor of mithai
The green script sign will catch your eye.

_____

_____

18

When you have sampled all of Devon's flavors
Siblings help you take some home to savor
Taste India's regional diversity
Through rice, pickles, parathas, and chutneys.

19

Looking for an Islamic read?
This shop is where you should proceed
There's books for kids and grown-ups, too
Fun education is their view.

Uptown and Andersonville

An entertainment powerhouse in the 1920s, the diverse Uptown community area still draws visitors to its live music and theater venues, historic architecture, and international food scene. This hunt also includes the nearby Andersonville neighborhood, an inviting enclave of small businesses, a proud LGBTQ community, and Swedish roots. Take the Red Line to Argyle station. Metered parking is available.

1

The lone local spot for Swedish cuisine
Patrons eat breakfast just like the Vikings
Try ordering the meatballs, and pickled herring,
Or pancakes topped with tart lingonberry.

2

A shop where reading is the aim
Community is in its name
Books for kids and feminist lit
Their author readings are a hit.

3

A water tower in yellow and blue
The Andersonville symbol welcomes you
A blue Dala horse is displayed inside
This collection of local ethnic pride.

4

You aren't drunk (yet) if you think,
"Is that a fish? Holding a drink?"
Visit the bar in wintertime
To sample tasty Swedish mulled wine.

_____

_____

5

You might smell a baking, savory pie
Coming from this corner as you walk by
Stock up on lentils or eat falafel
Either way you will leave with an armful.

_____

_____

6

The world's weirdest items are proudly featured
At this shop named for an ancient creature
From books to skeletons, this husband and wife
Help to give creepy objects a new life.

7

A place where beer geeks can drink and talk
Three leaves are hanging above the sidewalk
With Belgian-inspired food and brews
Mussels and frites you should choose.

8

Look for "misdirection" along Clark Street
(Just finding the entrance is a feat!)
Go in but leave your detergent behind
And prepare for these wizards to blow your mind.

_____

_____

9

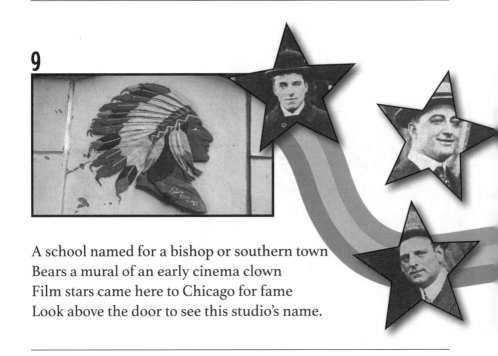

A school named for a bishop or southern town
Bears a mural of an early cinema clown
Film stars came here to Chicago for fame
Look above the door to see this studio's name.

_____

_____

10

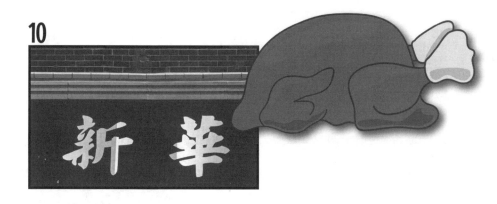

On Broadway, green tile sits above the sign
Birds in the window invite you to dine
Order off-menu and ask them to bring
Three courses of barbecue duck Beijing.

11

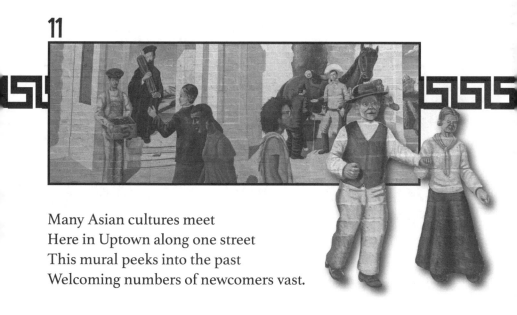

Many Asian cultures meet
Here in Uptown along one street
This mural peeks into the past
Welcoming numbers of newcomers vast.

Two granite sculptures will be your guide
To signal the artwork you'll find inside
While you wait there to mail a letter
Find the mural of a local writer.

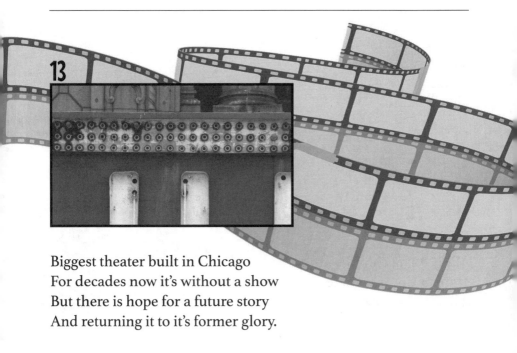

13

Biggest theater built in Chicago
For decades now it's without a show
But there is hope for a future story
And returning it to it's former glory.

14

'Neath this neon sign it's still the Jazz Age
The Poetry Slam was born on its stage
Where Billie and Ella blew off the roof
And Capone held court in the corner booth.

15

If African flavors are what you crave
This restaurant's reviews are all the rave
Your hands or injera bread do the job
Of scooping up platters of messob.

16

Built to resemble a castle in Spain
A giant neon marquee spells out its name
It hosted roller-skating and ballroom dance
Catch a rock concert if you have the chance.

17

It bears the same name as that of the street
This elegant lobby's the chic place to meet
During restoration, they discovered a pool
It's now a place to live that's uniquely cool.

18

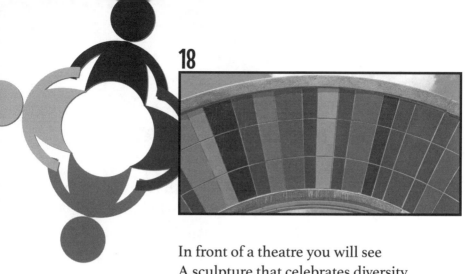

In front of a theatre you will see
A sculpture that celebrates diversity
More Chicago cultures than you know
Are honored together in this rainbow.

_____

_____

19

Uptown was a destination
When they built this Beaux Arts station
Now that it's been restored with pride
Admire it when you take a ride.

_____

_____

Lincoln Square

Charming Lincoln Square is located along the North Branch of the Chicago River. This community area with German roots offers old-world character among its modern boutiques, restaurants, and bakeries. You'll see one student carrying an instrument case for every two strollers in this village-like atmosphere. Take the Brown Line to Western station. Metered parking is available.

1

Resembling a castle more than a gate
Its design a Water Tower encore
Inside, souls rest who've met their fate
The grounds include a museum of war.

2

An inaugural brewer of crafts
Stop in to taste a draft
Pour a lager, a stout, or an IPA
Try Daisy Cutter or Gone Away.

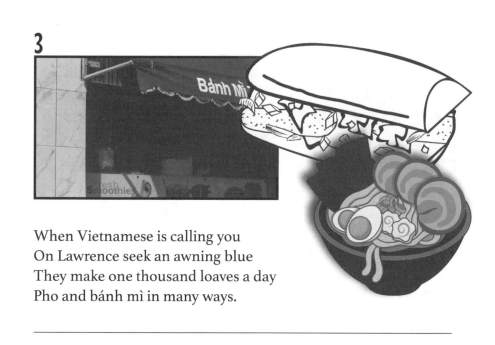

3

When Vietnamese is calling you
On Lawrence seek an awning blue
They make one thousand loaves a day
Pho and bánh mì in many ways.

4

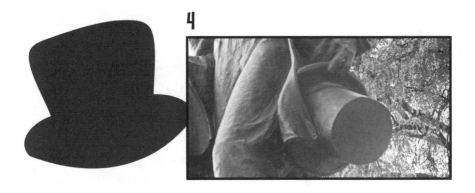

Here's a sculpture of this President
When he was an Illinois resident
His younger self holding books and a hat
Visit his plaza and have a chat.

5

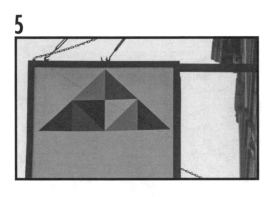

A flag waves on Western Avenue
Marking cultural artifacts you can view
Where much of the neighborhood has its roots
It's the country where they drink beer from boots.

6

The food in the name is not all they have
There's more beer and meats here than you can grab
A cow is the symbol of this Euro-style deli
Dine on the roof and fill up your belly.

_____

_____

7

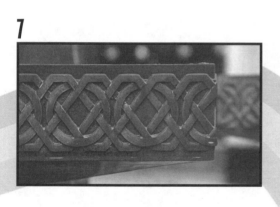

This public space got a new name
Its five squares bubble the same
Where a tall gift from Germany
Illuminates the walkway.

_____

_____

8

Seek out the oldest drugstore in town
A place where natural health goods abound
Stained glass and carved wood will tell you you're there
Stock up on herbal products and also skin care.

_____

_____

9

At Lincoln and Leland when you're walking by
It's blue and white and thirty-foot-high
A striking reminder of cultural traditions
Like the nearby mural's lasting mission.

_____

_____

10

1989

Look for a fragment around the station
For a symbol of a defunct nation
One side is plain, one covered in art
Gifted in gratitude for a fresh start.

_____

_____

11

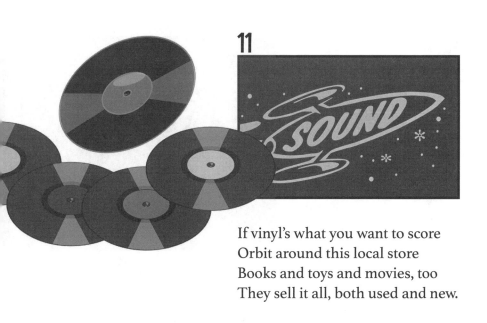

If vinyl's what you want to score
Orbit around this local store
Books and toys and movies, too
They sell it all, both used and new.

_____

_____

12

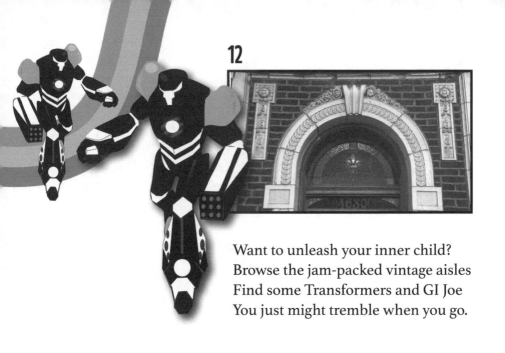

Want to unleash your inner child?
Browse the jam-packed vintage aisles
Find some Transformers and GI Joe
You just might tremble when you go.

13

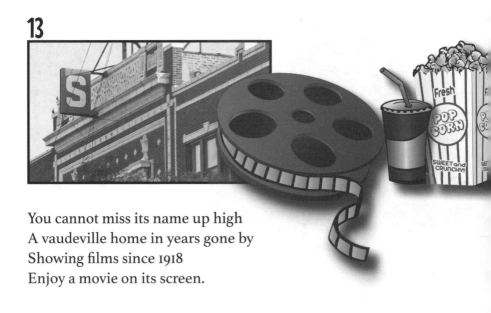

You cannot miss its name up high
A vaudeville home in years gone by
Showing films since 1918
Enjoy a movie on its screen.

14

Look here for Sullivan's last design
On a building used for instrument sales
Where the unique green terra-cotta shines
Ornate geometric and nature details.

15

When you spot the owl, c'mon in!
For budding musicians, it's the place to begin
Banjo and accordion are just two
Of the musical skills they can teach you.

16

Across the park you'll see a dome
It's named after a pioneer
Thousands of books call this place home
You'll find local archives inside here.

_____

_____

17

You'll see a gazebo standing near
On logs and stones children play here
A garden and a council ring
Encourage outdoor exploring.

_____

_____

18

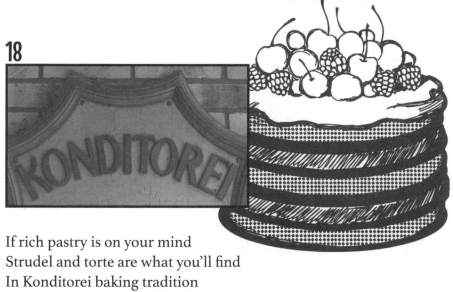

If rich pastry is on your mind
Strudel and torte are what you'll find
In Konditorei baking tradition
European methods are their mission.

_____

_____

19

Near the Chicago River and Montrose
Lies a park that only the community knows
Native species line this riverwalk
Now it's accessible for all to flock.

_____

_____

Lake View

Lake View, also spelled Lakeview, is a hub for entertainment located along Lake Michigan on Chicago's North Side. Lake View delivers fun for everyone, from the sports bars of Wrigleyville to the LBGTQ-friendly clubs of Northalsted (formerly Boystown), theaters, and music venues. This hunt also features an historic cemetery that borders the neighborhood. Take the Red Line to Addison station. Metered parking is available.

1

In a resting place, this haunting, cloaked fright
Guards a hotelier, an eerie sight
Forever quiet, the work's name implies
A legend warns not to look in its eyes.

On Main Avenue a surprise can be seen
A sphinx and an angel holding a key
Guarding the portal to a grand pyramid
He made his fortune on tempting liquid.

Seek out a temple on the lake
With two sarcophagi tucked inside
A hotel is this man's namesake
Joined by Chicago's queen, his bride.

4

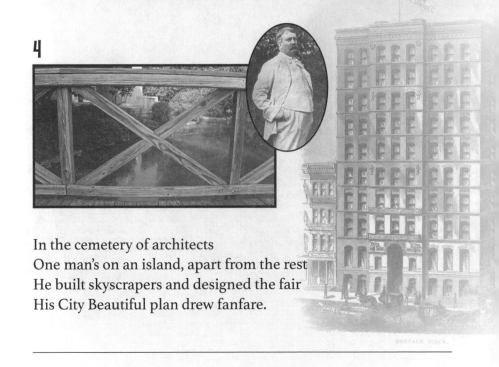

In the cemetery of architects
One man's on an island, apart from the rest
He built skyscrapers and designed the fair
His City Beautiful plan drew fanfare.

_____

_____

5

On Lake Avenue find a green bronze door
A limestone box decked in ornate decor
This Chicago Landmark delights the eye
Its iconic designer rests nearby.

_____

_____

6

Atop this marker, home plate and a glove
Honor the resting place of "Mr. Cub"
A Hall-of-Famer who said, "Let's play two"
At the ballpark you can view his statue.

_____

_____

7

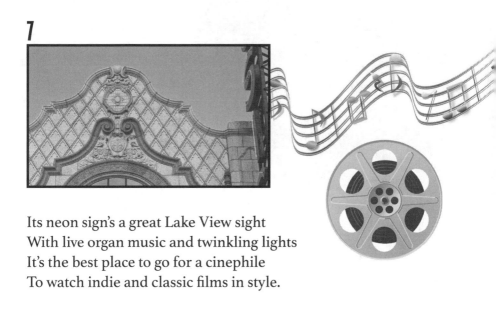

Its neon sign's a great Lake View sight
With live organ music and twinkling lights
It's the best place to go for a cinephile
To watch indie and classic films in style.

_____

_____

8

If farm-to-table is what you want
Here's America's "Greenest Restaurant"
The first organic brewery in the state
Vegan and gluten-removed beers are great!

9

Just two blocks north of the Friendly Confines
Is a street of intriguing home designs
London row houses make you see double
Finding these twins shouldn't be too much trouble.

10

This rock club's stage gets the music pumpin'
From Chance the Rapper to Smashing Pumpkins
In the basement dance the night away
To top international, electronic DJs.

11

Found by the cheap seats, "Holy Cow!"
This announcer really knew how to wow
While you stretch, remember his name
Sing, "Take Me Out to the Ballgame."

12

Corner on Halsted look above the door
To see what this building was before
City center when Lake View was on its own
LGBTQ seniors now call it home.

13

A grand clock tower leads the way
To a scenic little park cafe
But back behind it, that's not all
There's a great place to hit some balls.

14

A colorful thunderbird, spreading its wings
Is one of Chicago's more surprising things
A copy of a piece which once stood here
The original's been gone for many a year.

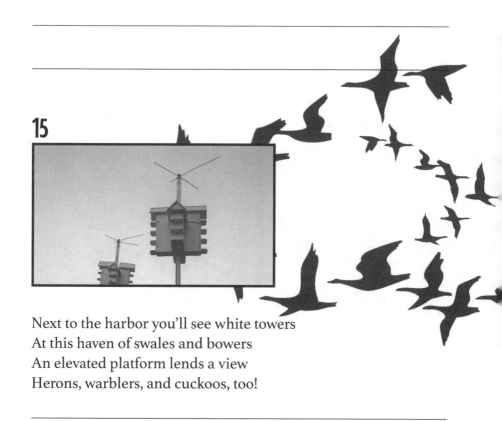

15

Next to the harbor you'll see white towers
At this haven of swales and bowers
An elevated platform lends a view
Herons, warblers, and cuckoos, too!

16

It's known as Northalsted today
Where rainbow pylons line the way
Through queer history these plaques will guide
In a neighborhood that's filled with pride.

_____

_____

17

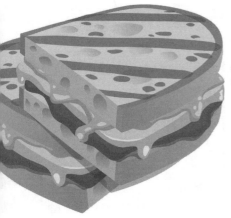

A restaurant ahead of the times
Their slogan already rhymes
Reubens of seitan they make
Just don't miss the vegan milkshake!

_____

_____

18

Along a harbor at the southern end
A giant figure jumps at the center
This garden honoring departed friends
Learning and healing for those who enter.

19

The largest theater district isn't the Loop
Fifty theaters around Belmont is proof
Subversive comedy is at this one
The big cocktail marks the place for fun.

20

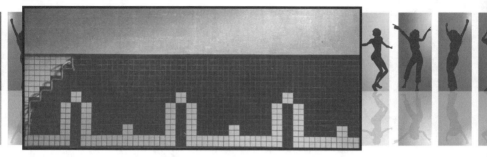

Pan cultural dance parties since '83
Whether gay, straight, trans, or nonbinary
Named after a city once split in two
Come as you are, the dance floor welcomes you.

21

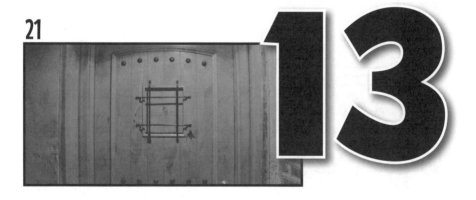

There's a secret at this B&B
You'll need the code word to pop in and see
A speakeasy entrance is your mission
Lindy Hop back into Prohibition.

22

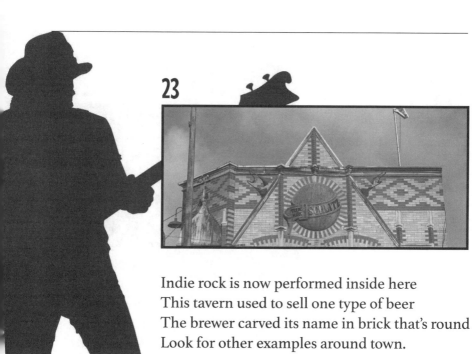

Oakdale was home to barons of clay
You'll see their product is still on display
With ornate ornament these homes are brimming
Look on the west for a woman spinning.

23

Indie rock is now performed inside here
This tavern used to sell one type of beer
The brewer carved its name in brick that's round
Look for other examples around town.

Lincoln Park

Home to Chicago's largest park, it's easy to see why picturesque and historic Lincoln Park is so popular. Once a cemetery, the namesake park attracts visitors with its lush green space and lakefront access. Take the Red, Brown, or Purple Line to Fullerton station. Metered parking is available.

1

At every entrance, take a look
You'll think you're in a storybook
Seek out whimsical sculptures four
You're not in Kansas anymore . . .

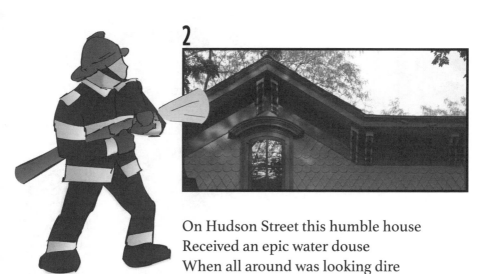

2

On Hudson Street this humble house
Received an epic water douse
When all around was looking dire
It survived the Great Chicago Fire.

3

Two regal brothers guard the door
Steeped in symbols of ancient lore
King Tut himself would sure approve
Of their mission to help you move.

4

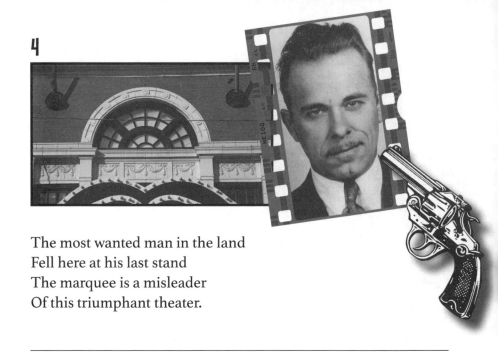

The most wanted man in the land
Fell here at his last stand
The marquee is a misleader
Of this triumphant theater.

_____

_____

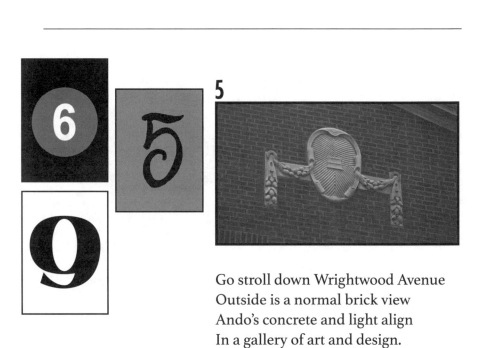

5

Go stroll down Wrightwood Avenue
Outside is a normal brick view
Ando's concrete and light align
In a gallery of art and design.

_____

_____

6

A hospital once sat on this site
Now it's a condo of impressive height
A holy place is hidden away
For the first saint from the USA.

7

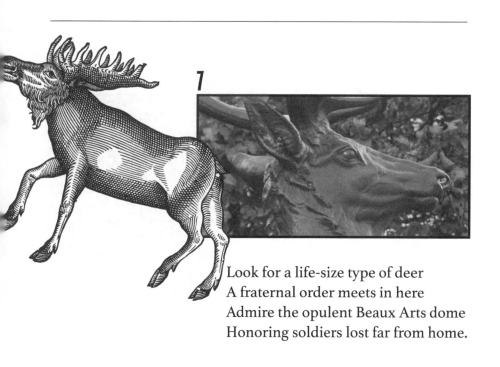

Look for a life-size type of deer
A fraternal order meets in here
Admire the opulent Beaux Arts dome
Honoring soldiers lost far from home.

8

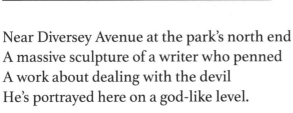

Near Diversey Avenue at the park's north end
A massive sculpture of a writer who penned
A work about dealing with the devil
He's portrayed here on a god-like level.

_____

_____

9

Watch out for roots above the ground
Sharing the local wildlife's tales
Hundreds of flapping wings are found
Also, bird walks and nature trails.

_____

_____

10

Tucked off a busy avenue
An oasis to disappear into
It's Prairie Style right at a glance
Plus a secret garden with native plants.

_____

_____

11

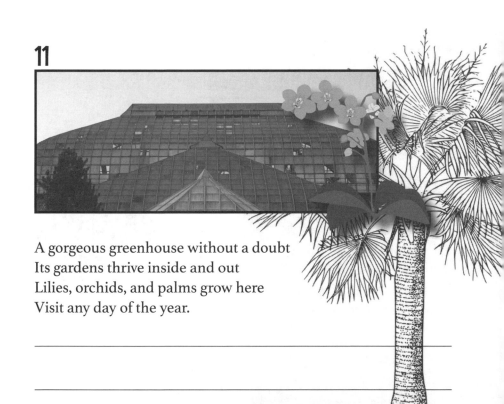

A gorgeous greenhouse without a doubt
Its gardens thrive inside and out
Lilies, orchids, and palms grow here
Visit any day of the year.

_____

_____

12

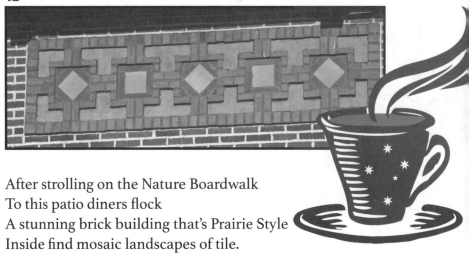

After strolling on the Nature Boardwalk
To this patio diners flock
A stunning brick building that's Prairie Style
Inside find mosaic landscapes of tile.

_____

_____

13

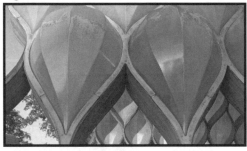

Poised along the South Pond wetland
A structure rises that's truly grand
Is it a turtle shell? Or a honeycomb?
Ponder as this scenic area you roam.

_____

_____

14

One of Chicago's more colorful names
A Boston Tea Partier among other claims
He was buried here, or so it would seem
At the very ripe age of 115.

15

Not far from South Pond along Stockton Drive
The ridge of an ancient sand bar survives
Ages ago water was where you stand
A marker shows where the lake met the land.

16

On the history trail this hunk of stone
Formed from rock, molten iron, and brick
The worst of disasters the city has known
Proof of resilience lies in this relic.

17

A resting place now used by athletes
One reminder of what's 'neath their feet
The door is sealed and no records provide
Who or how many are buried inside.

18

Park and neighborhood's namesake
A speech he is about to make
Our leader in times of greatest strife
An honored figure who's larger than life.

19

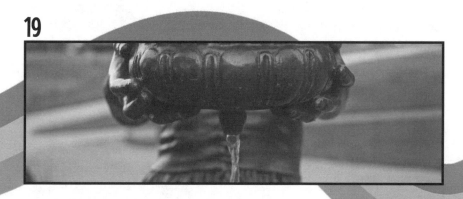

Not far from the previous clue
Chicago's barefoot daughter
With arms outstretched she offers you
A cool trickling source of water.

Near North Side

The Near North Side is a collection of tony neighborhoods just north of the Loop. From the vintage charm of Old Town and the Gold Coast to the chic shopping and dining of Streeterville and River North, it offers plenty of ways to spend your money. Home to Gilded Age architecture and Modernist icons alike, there's no shortage of history to explore. Take the Red Line to Chicago station. Metered street parking and paid garages are available.

1

"Am I in Japan?" you'll wonder
Seeing this place to practice Shin
Dedicated to its founders
Is a peaceful hidden garden.

2

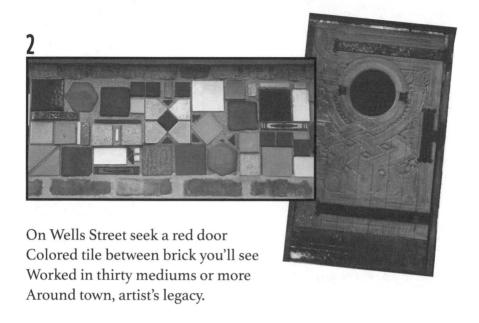

On Wells Street seek a red door
Colored tile between brick you'll see
Worked in thirty mediums or more
Around town, artist's legacy.

Freundschaft und Freiheit

3

Across from Oliver on Crilly Court
Site of the first group for gay rights support
He formed the Society for Human Rights
In Rogers Park his name's memorialized.

4

Four Old Town faces cast in stone
Came from a German theater
Displayed where comedy is shown
Discover the next big star here.

5

Stroll down this lane and you will see
A most unusual use of a tree
No stone is found beneath your feet
Close to where the Cardinal sleeps.

6

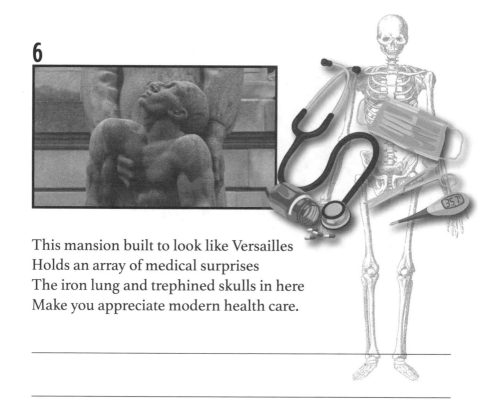

This mansion built to look like Versailles
Holds an array of medical surprises
The iron lung and trephined skulls in here
Make you appreciate modern health care.

7

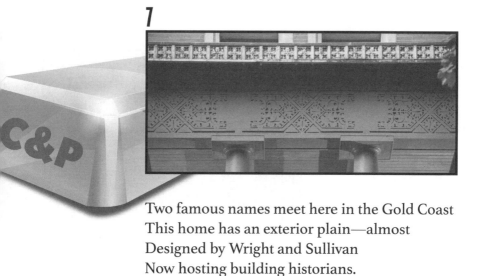

Two famous names meet here in the Gold Coast
This home has an exterior plain—almost
Designed by Wright and Sullivan
Now hosting building historians.

8

A place for female artists to reside
Now fancy furniture is sold inside
Find stone reliefs of women displayed
Then enjoy a meal in the scenic cafe.

_____

_____

9

This park shares its name with one in NYC
Close by a fountain and research library
A marker notes this nickname of free speech
Radical thinkers gathered here to preach.

_____

_____

10

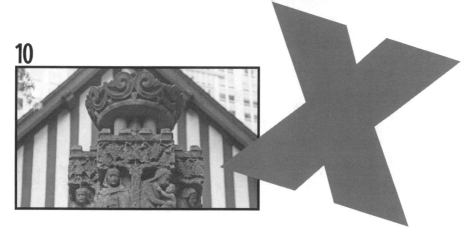

At one skyscraper X marks the spot
Across the street solace is sought
Just past the arches sits a courtyard
Relax where a gentle trickling is heard.

11

A glorified pipe for water pressure
Is a symbolic Chicago treasure
Now this "castellated monstrosity"
Holds an unexpected art gallery.

12

Outside, it's like a big black box
Thousands of volumes of books it stocks
Focusing on one writing style
Stop in sometime and read here for awhile.

_____

_____

13

A lake shares its name with this street
This grand mansion is not discreet
Restored to Gilded Age glory
Art exhibits tell its story.

_____

_____

14

Named after a holy city
This domed brick building is pretty
Used by Shriners and a home store
Arabic script surrounds the door.

15

"One" is included right in the name
Inventing deep dish is their claim to fame
If a long line here makes you frown
Go and try "two" just a block down.

16

A gold dome above the Magnificent Mile
For flying machines that went out of style
Medinah Athletic Club was its name
Above neo-Egyptian scenes are framed.

_____

_____

17

This old man in bronze managed to evade
The city and his neighbors for three decades
He washed ashore and without shame
Built a shantytown that bears his name.

_____

_____

18

This impressive show of waterpower
Makes a splash of ninety feet each hour
From a grand waterfall it flows in tiers
Marking aquatic feats of one hundred years.

_____

_____

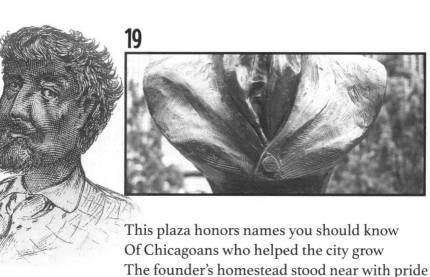

19

This plaza honors names you should know
Of Chicagoans who helped the city grow
The founder's homestead stood near with pride
You will find his bust by the riverside.

_____

_____

20

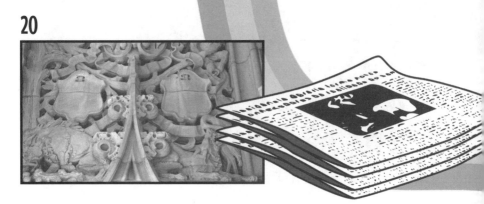

Winning design of Gothic acclaim
Once filled with journalistic pride
See fragments brought from places of fame
Like Paris meeting the North Side.

_____

_____

21

Next to the building named for gum
There is a peaceful place to come
Here an heroic Mexican stands
On a street lined with flags from distant lands.

_____

_____

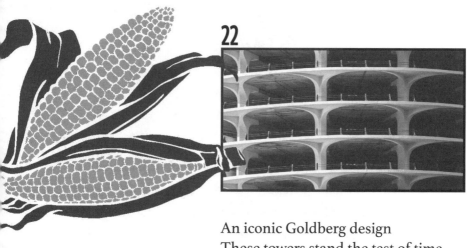

22

An iconic Goldberg design
These towers stand the test of time
Curves like flower petals or corn
The Hunter sent a car airborne.

23

To commercial center from trading post
"Amongst the world's largest" is no idle boast
With names that spread throughout the land
These eight giants gaze but they don't stand.

Loop

Named for its elevated train tracks, the Loop is Chicago's downtown. The area that began with a couple of houses and a fort on the river originated the skyscraper, the department store, and many other historic moments. Chicago's central business district boasts lakefront parks, theaters, and iconic architecture—there's more to the Loop than you think. Take any CTA train to downtown. Paid garages are available.

Stop near the bridge, then take a look down
To glimpse the site that became our town
Early residents didn't get far
It since became Chicago's first star.

2

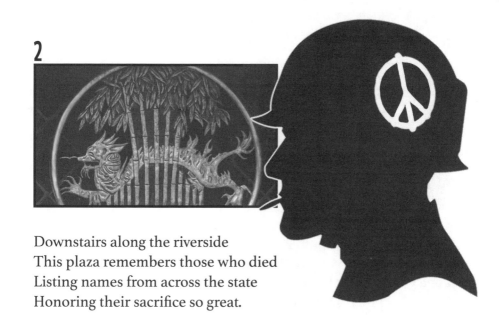

Downstairs along the riverside
This plaza remembers those who died
Listing names from across the state
Honoring their sacrifice so great.

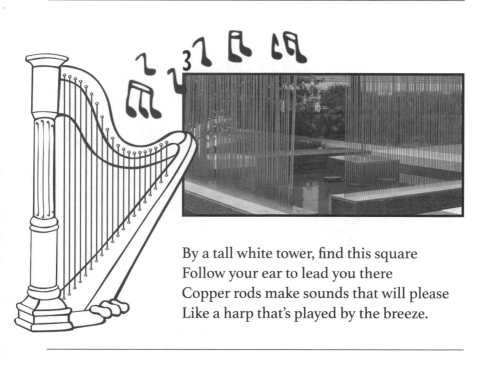

By a tall white tower, find this square
Follow your ear to lead you there
Copper rods make sounds that will please
Like a harp that's played by the breeze.

4

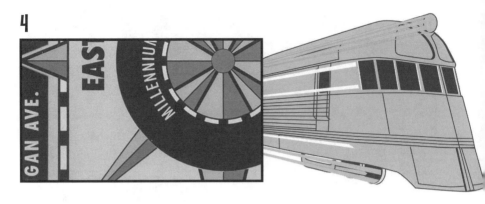

When you're in the Loop look around
For a compass rose symbol in gold
For a guide through the underground
Five miles safe from heat and cold.

5

A seven-ton gathering place
Roman numerals on the face
Chicagoans have said "meet here"
For well over one hundred years.

6

Across from Picasso look for a man
Who's boldly grabbed lightning bolts by the hand
A plain-looking building to you or me
It provides Chicago's electricity.

7

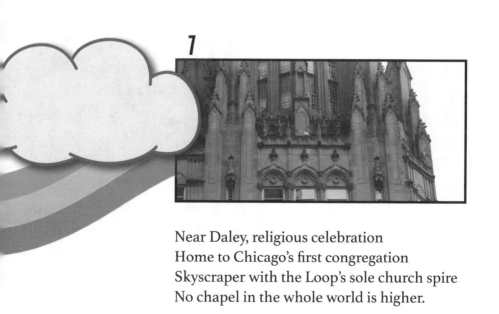

Near Daley, religious celebration
Home to Chicago's first congregation
Skyscraper with the Loop's sole church spire
No chapel in the whole world is higher.

8

Look up for a dazzling sight
Of father and son taking flight
A warning close by City Hall
"Pride always comes before a fall."

9

Near where river branches meet
Look for a plaque right in the street
Once the site of a national convention
Where our own man won the nomination.

10

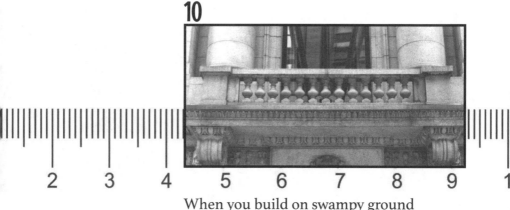

2   3   4   5   6   7   8   9   1

When you build on swampy ground
How do you survey heights around?
This bedrock benchmarks city heights
And shares its name with famous lights.

_____

_____

11

Burnham, Root, and Frank Lloyd Wright
Had a part in this grand Moorish sight
Named for where nesting birds lay
A clue is carved by the entryway.

_____

_____

12

Two buildings—face-to-face—are twins
One's Ionic but you want Corinthian
Here, major railroad companies designed
Our time zone standards that are still assigned.

13

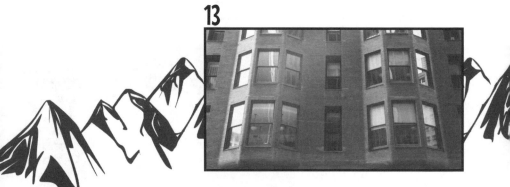

Tallest load-bearing building of brick
No ornament on its walls so thick
The other half was built with steel frame
An eastern mountain is in its name.

14

A place you go for government
Mies made a black steel and glass scene
This striking scarlet piece is bent
Like no bird you have ever seen.

15

This building shares a priest's name
His story's above the doorframe
Inside, see the lobby shine
With colorful Tiffany designs.

16

The corner from which all roads lead
Once nicknamed "the world's busiest street"
Iron botanicals adorn the doorway
The designer's initials are also displayed.

_____

_____

17

You can't miss fifty-foot-tall Chicagoans
They're old and young in every shade of skin
Like modern gargoyles, their faces pout
And out of their lips spray waterspouts!

_____

_____

18

East of the lions, find a portal to the past
A remnant from a building that didn't last
Salvaging this space, sadly, one man died
Now, its trading room is preserved inside.

19

Just outside of art's hallowed walls
Five bronze maidens carry water
And from each woman's shell it falls
Like lakes into one another.

20

By DePaul look for an alley
You'll wake up and smell the coffee
Former stable and restaurant
A quaint little lane that time forgot.

21

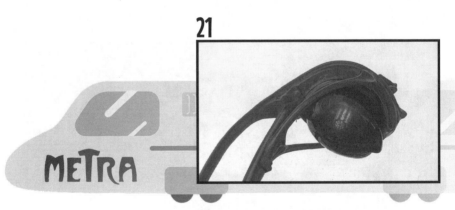

Walking along Van Buren Street
You'll think you're in gay Paree
This reproduced Art Nouveau sight
Is a gift from the City of Lights.

22

On Michigan Ave. arches in a row
Painters, dancers, and instruments that blow
A theater built as a carriage store
Its creative name is above the door.

23

Warriors on horses guard an entry
Recalling Chicago's past as prairie
The duo was sculpted by a famed Croatian
Their weapons left to the imagination.

24

Look for *Harmony* to locate the start
To this living urban canvas of art
Artists were asked to leave their impression
A celebration of creative expression.

25

You're damn right, he has the blues
And at this corner you can, too
Living legends come to hear him play
With hot blues artists of today.

26

This building was home to the printing trade
As its mural by Oskar Gross displayed
Artist to engraver the progression
Creating a book, *The First Impression*.

27

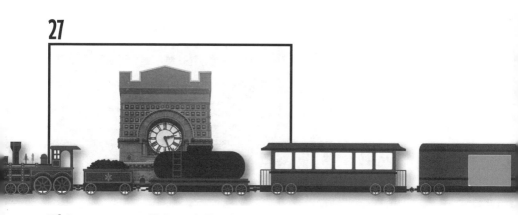

This tower over Printer's Row
Where now you come to see a jazz show
It once greeted trains rolling into town
Like Super Chief and El Capitan.

28

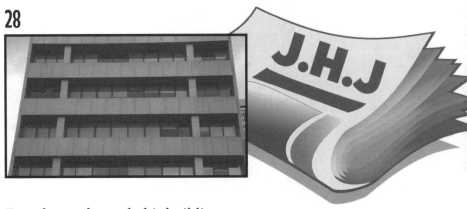

Found near the park this building matters
The first Loop high-rise by a Black architect
How fitting to see that it looks like a ladder
It housed Black culture like *Ebony* and *Jet*.

_____

_____

29

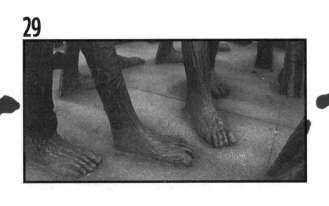

Passersby will stop here and gawk
At sculptures that seem to walk the walk
Named for a central meeting place
Above their legs there's only space.

_____

_____

30

Just steps away from the previous clue
Find decorative granite fragments two
These welcomed thousands as part of a station
Arriving during the Great Migration.

_____

_____

Near West Side

Just west of the Loop, the Near West Side is a community area encompassing a cluster of neighborhoods. Traditional restaurants, bakeries, and businesses still dot the ethnic enclaves of Little Italy and Greektown. In the formerly industrial West Loop and Fulton Market, meatpacking facilities gave way to foodie havens and corporate headquarters. Take the Blue Line to UIC-Halsted station. Metered parking is available.

1

From musical tributes and the like
To an elephant riding on a bike
The mile-long embankment on this street
Is a colorful gallery that can't be beat!

2

You're not imagining that chocolatey scent
This clue requires you to follow your nose
From Halsted to the river, the smell descends
They're roasting cocoa for the candy pros.

_____

_____

3

Find a taste of Paris on Clinton Street
When you head to the place where train lines meet
Thirty vendors are in this food hall
From macarons to bánh mì, you must try them all.

_____

_____

The speaker's wagon stood right on this spot
For an eight-hour workday activists fought
Sadly, that meeting had a tragic ending
While their free speech and assembly they were defending.

_____

_____

5

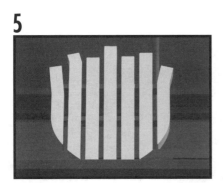

Golden arches among the glass and steel
They signal the spot to get a cheap meal
From Brazil to Hong Kong, it's the venue
To sample Ronald's global menu.

_____

_____

6

Back when meatpacking was the West Loop's trade
This building is where the sausage was made
Art Deco in terra cotta and much, much more
Its name is still carved right over the door.

7

Near this giant yellow door where you stand
You'll think you've arrived in Wonderland
A green creature stands lookout from inside
Where fun ideas are brought to life.

8

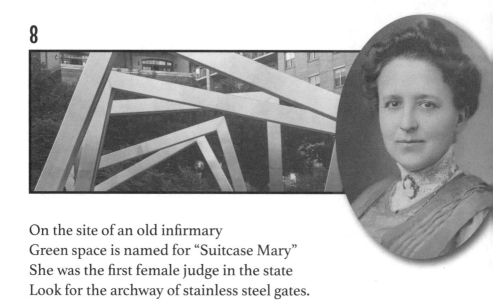

On the site of an old infirmary
Green space is named for "Suitcase Mary"
She was the first female judge in the state
Look for the archway of stainless steel gates.

9

A Greektown business for one hundred years
Their neon sign isn't all that glows
They hand-dip beeswax tapers in here
Four generations have helped it grow.

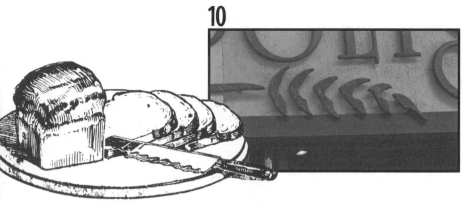

10

Part of this bistro's sign means "bread"
"City" is also in its name
Don't miss baklava for your spread
Artopitas is their dish of fame.

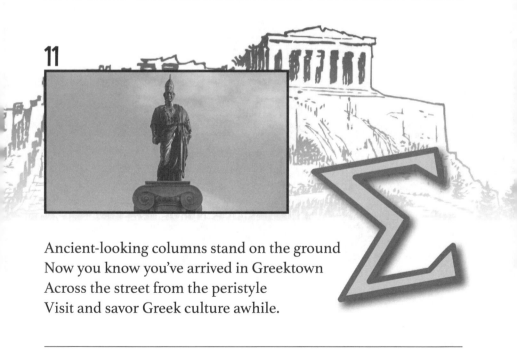

11

Ancient-looking columns stand on the ground
Now you know you've arrived in Greektown
Across the street from the peristyle
Visit and savor Greek culture awhile.

12

It's the oldest public building in town
Mismatched spires honor East and West
Survived the fire when blocks away burned down
Ireland's saint must have deemed it blessed.

_____

_____

13

Bargain hunters flock from near and far
To score deals in this open-air bazaar
The original was displaced by UIC
The start of Chicago blues history.

_____

_____

14

The only address you'll find on this street
Is where trainees learn to beat the heat
The Great Fire's origin is marked by a bronze flame
Mrs. O'Leary's cow took the blame.

15

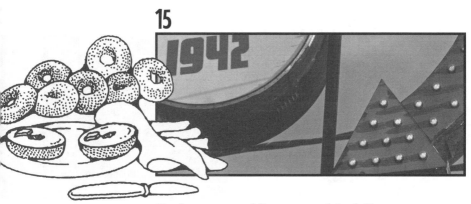

Grab a tray and line up at this deli
For Jewish comfort food to fill your belly
It's been family-run for eighty years
Serving corned beef and bagels with a schmear.

16

Did a flying saucer land at UIC?
Nope—it's just an observatory
Visit and look up at sunset or sunrise
To admire the artwork that is the night sky.

_____

_____

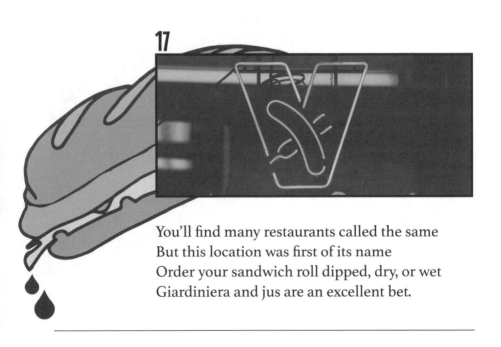

17

You'll find many restaurants called the same
But this location was first of its name
Order your sandwich roll dipped, dry, or wet
Giardiniera and jus are an excellent bet.

_____

_____

18

When you can't stand the summer heat
Go get in line on Taylor Street
This tiny stand has a tiny price
To cool you off with delicious shaved ice.

19

This home's wide veranda welcomes you
As it has for thousands of immigrants before
It now preserves this activist's view
Of supporting and providing services for the poor.

West Town

The West Town community area has been shaped by immigrant groups from around the world. Encompassing eclectic neighborhoods like Wicker Park, Bucktown, Noble Square, and Ukrainian Village, West Town is a hub of creativity. Shop for vintage finds, grab a craft cocktail, and catch some live music. Take the Blue Line to Division station. Free and metered parking is available.

1

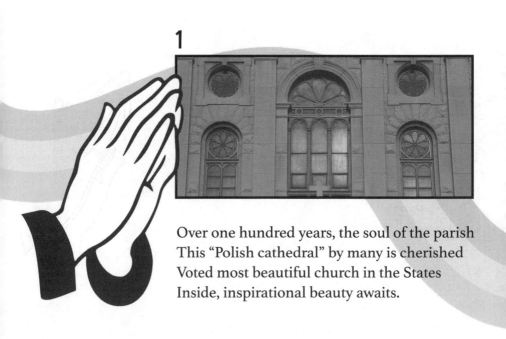

Over one hundred years, the soul of the parish
This "Polish cathedral" by many is cherished
Voted most beautiful church in the States
Inside, inspirational beauty awaits.

2

A wolf on a leash on the outside brick
Inside, no work from the mainstream art clique
Self-taught and marginalized creators bloom
Like Vivian Girls artist's replica room.

_____

_____

3

Try to find Chi-Town's smallest bar
Beside an out-of-place, railroad car
Bourdain ate here after it rode the rails
Today you can toast with classic cocktails.

_____

_____

4

A nickelodeon with a silent screen
Is how it opened in 1918
This storefront has a musical name
Offering avant-garde art is their aim.

5

Wicker Park's most acclaimed writer
Honored here with falling water
His words are spelled out on the ground
At Polonia Triangle it can be found.

6

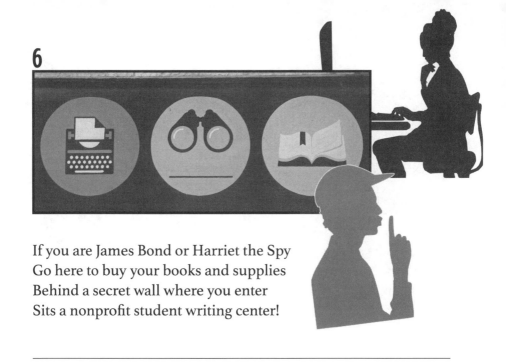

If you are James Bond or Harriet the Spy
Go here to buy your books and supplies
Behind a secret wall where you enter
Sits a nonprofit student writing center!

_____

_____

7

Down the block from the Augusta angel
One artist's work has a playful angle
It's a metallic mound that you can bet
Reminds owners to scoop after their pets.

_____

_____

8

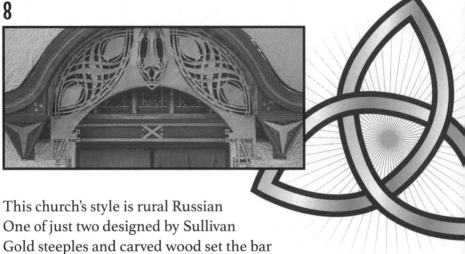

This church's style is rural Russian
One of just two designed by Sullivan
Gold steeples and carved wood set the bar
It was partially paid for by the czar.

_____

_____

9

This home is on Evergreen Avenue
Part of the street has another name, too
Where the author portrayed a life that's gritty
"On the Make" is what he called the city.

_____

_____

At its heart lies triangular space
A Gurgoyle replica flows in its place
A man with a broom stands in bronze acclaim
He gave both land and the area his name.

11

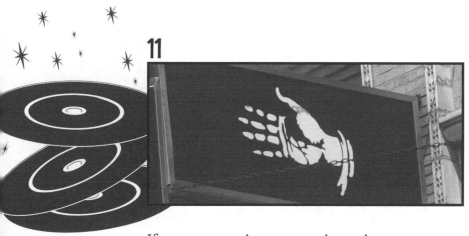

If you want to give new music a spin
Look for the outstretched hand and walk in
Flip through the stacks where vinyl still thrives
You might see musicians performing live.

12

A colorful corner archway that glows
Classic local architecture it shows
These modest brick homes of the working class
The blue-collar neighborhood of years past.

A mural honoring Black history
Thirty feet tall along the Blue Line train
The image from a Memphis tragedy
His sign is still a civil rights refrain.

14

She holds a camera on North Avenue
An artist in her lifetime, but nobody knew
She captured Chicago's mid century
Now her work is celebrated—finally.

15

A two-headed mouse reads above the door
Of this delightfully quirky independent bookstore
Alternative comics and mags are seen
And they specialize in stocking zines.

16

A Wicker Park landmark that's now a hotel
Art Deco, and once called the Coyote as well
An early skyscraper set outside downtown
Its rooftop offers views for miles around.

_____

_____

17

Roam the street that's nicknamed Beer Baron Row
And look for a surprise in one yard that's meant to blow
The site of a former American Legion hall
This one never answered the battle call.

_____

_____

18

Walk, bike, or jog down this old freight rail
Also known as the Bloomingdale Trail
Seventeen feet up, a neighborhood tour
You're on one bridge, yet below another.

19

Named for the market and tavern owner
Downstairs she ran a secret rathskeller
This Bucktown bar has been seen on TV
Stop in for a cold one at the place called Molly's.

Logan Square

Logan Square is a community area located along Chicago's scenic boulevard system. The trendy area is home to an always-evolving restaurant and bar scene. Explore the old greystones and latest nightlife. Take the Blue Line to California station. Free and metered parking is available.

1

Part ice cream parlor and part candy store
It's famous for welcoming England's Fab Four
Down Western Ave. its neon lights the way
Order a split or atomic sundae.

_____

_____

2

Honoring a Chicagoan's memory
He sang, "You never had a friend like me"
This comic's work made laughter fill the room
Sadly, his talent left the world too soon.

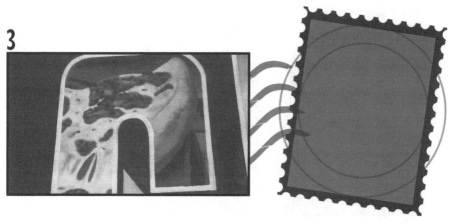

3

It's painted near the Blue Line tracks
This postcard shows you where you're at
Muddy and Ferris are a few
Of the local icons that welcome you.

4

The state's largest indy brewery
Is known for its on-tap variety
IPAs, Pilsners, Belgians, and ales
This labor of love has won them strong sales.

5

On a street that's named for a town
Diamonds made of bricks can be found
Ready to play? They've got it all
Try pool, air hockey, and vintage pinball.

6

When you're ready to get rollin'
Head this way toward the giant pin
You may catch a rock and roll show
Or score a turkey with your throw.

7

Located in a circle on the square
All roads in the neighborhood lead to there
From a Doric order an eagle peers
Celebrating the state's first hundred years.

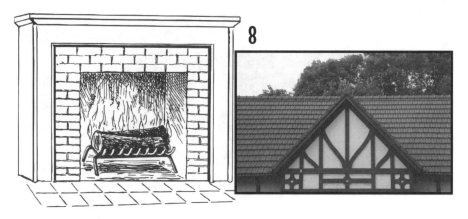

8

Once you've solved the prior clue
Find a Tudor building near you
Once used to warm up in the park
Now it's a home for modern art.

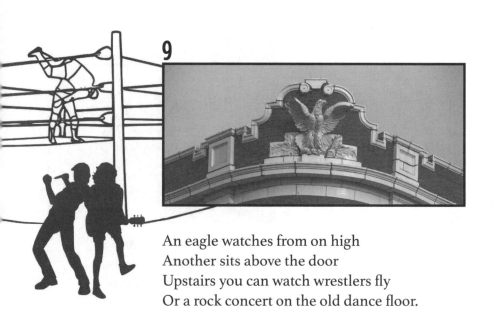

9

An eagle watches from on high
Another sits above the door
Upstairs you can watch wrestlers fly
Or a rock concert on the old dance floor.

10

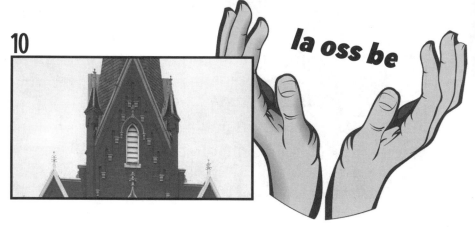

Red bricks and a steeple will guide the way
To an area once known as Little Norway
It's also known as a Minnekirken
A place to hear a mass in Norwegian.

_____

_____

11

The popular Logan Square location
Is the subject of gentrification
A mural near L train and bus lines
Depicts the neighbors at a moment in time.

_____

_____

12

Its name recalls a general
Spelled out in letters really tall
First features seen here had no sound
But now the latest flicks are found.

13

This church is not quite what it seems
A place to chase your big-top dreams
Train on aerial silks and trapeze
To fly through the air with the greatest of ease.

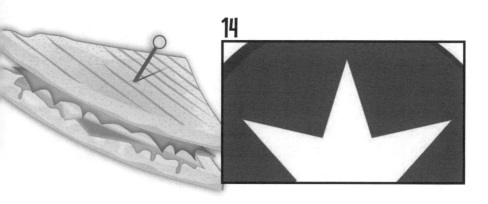

14

Puerto Rico inspired formation
Of this Chicago plantain creation
On Fullerton Avenue, find the door
To enjoy this tasty sandwich and more.

_____

_____

15

The boulevards are lined with stately homes
The "Emerald Necklace" is how they are known
The stone manor marked with a cross and crown
Is a temple where you can party down.

_____

_____

16

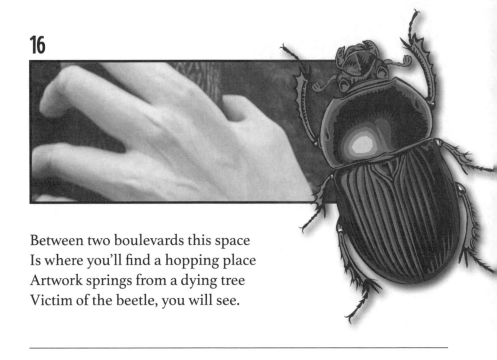

Between two boulevards this space
Is where you'll find a hopping place
Artwork springs from a dying tree
Victim of the beetle, you will see.

_____

_____

17

A vivid mural with a guitar
Marks this lively musical bar
Where Billy Branch and Sugar Blue
Look forward to serenading you.

_____

_____

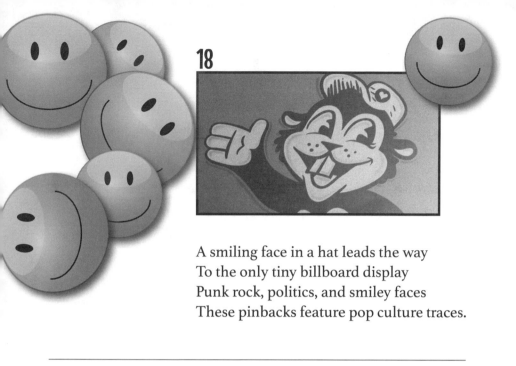

18

A smiling face in a hat leads the way
To the only tiny billboard display
Punk rock, politics, and smiley faces
These pinbacks feature pop culture traces.

19

The author who lived here dreamt a up world
With a scarecrow, lion, and lost girl
Boulevard where golden bricks pave the way
There's no place like home is what they do say.

South Loop

Just south of downtown, the captivating South Loop offers something for everyone. Over the years, the area has been home to the mansions of wealthy Chicagoans, railroad yards, a vice district, and an auto industry mecca. These days, its lakefront location draws visitors to historic neighborhoods, buzzing restaurants and entertainment venues, international conventions, thrilling sporting events, and cultural attractions. Take the Green Line to Cermak-McCormick Place station. Metered street parking and paid garages are available.

1

You'll think you landed in Jurassic Park
On arriving at this natural history landmark
But don't fear the creature that's forty-feet tall
It's not real bones, just a replica, that's all.

2

The Shedd Aquarium made a splash
When it installed this giant catch
A very tall man shows his feelings
For the care of aquatic beings.

_____

_____

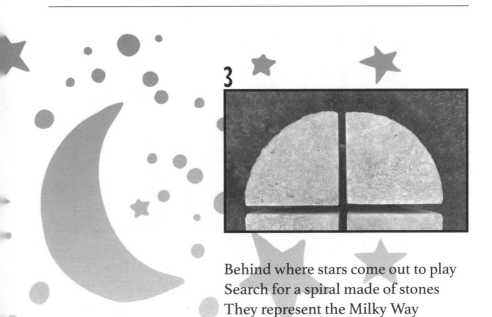

3

Behind where stars come out to play
Search for a spiral made of stones
They represent the Milky Way
And the diversity of our home.

_____

_____

4

It's where the whole world once was found
Now an oasis of paths and a pond
It looks like where you catch a flight
Start here to learn about the sights.

<hr />

5

Just north of the Monsters of the Midway
You'll find a flame burning bright each day
The birthplace of some special games was here
A monument to inclusion, hope, and cheer.

6

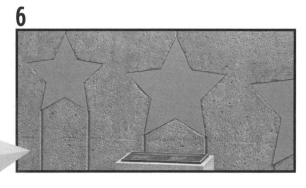

The checkered pattern of this waterfall
Like the hatband of those who gave their all
Over five hundred names here cast, the cost
In the line of duty their lives were lost.

_____

_____

7

This marker sparks controversy
A gift from fascist Italy
A temple relic two thousand years old
Piece of history to behold.

_____

_____

8

A park that marks an historic event
Where over fifty lives were spent
Fort residents who were on the run
And clashed with Native Americans.

9

Near other mansions this fortress of stone
Is Richardsonian, a class of its own
A foundation was founded to make it last
Here you can peek into lives of the past.

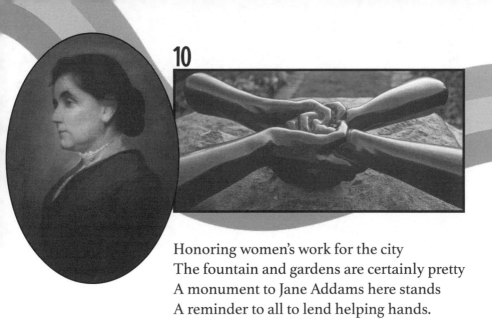

10

Honoring women's work for the city
The fountain and gardens are certainly pretty
A monument to Jane Addams here stands
A reminder to all to lend helping hands.

11

It is known as the oldest house in town
Bishop Ford's preservation is renowned
Once moved on a flatbed across the city
It shows what life was like on the prairie.

12

A national landmark on Michigan
By the designer of the Smithsonian
From the limestone tower gargoyles spy
Tiffany glass windows stun inside.

_____

_____

13

Rolling Stones named a song for this address
It was once the recording home of Chess
Featuring legends like Etta and Muddy
Preserving Chicago's famed blues legacy.

_____

_____

14

When this restaurant came to Chicago
The design was inspired by a tower you know
The oldest location still serves entrees
Once burgers, but it cooks much more today.

15

Before we had the automobile show
You would go car shopping on Motor Row
Dealers and shops from auto's golden age
Look for the building adorned with an "H."

16

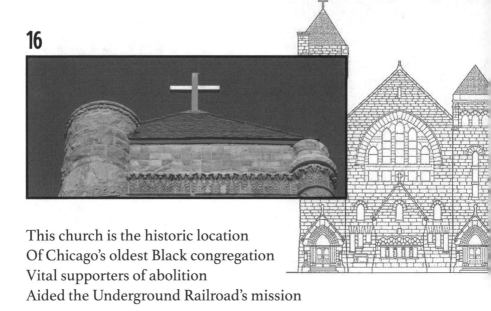

This church is the historic location
Of Chicago's oldest Black congregation
Vital supporters of abolition
Aided the Underground Railroad's mission

17

Seek a clock tower to find a hub
Once the Illinois Automobile Club
For decades after that it was used
To publish African American news.

18

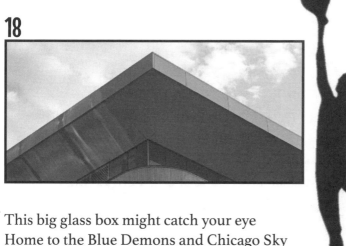

This big glass box might catch your eye
Home to the Blue Demons and Chicago Sky
A house on this site had to move
Over to Prairie Avenue.

19

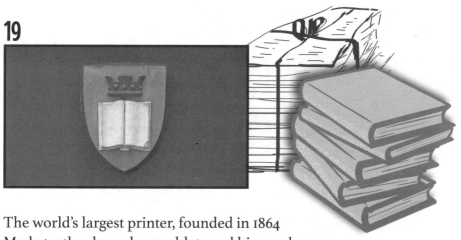

The world's largest printer, founded in 1864
Made textbooks and pamphlets and bios and more.
Time and *Life* were printed behind the plant door.
Outside, find carvings of shields 'mongst the decor.

Chinatown

Stepping into this century-old South Side neighborhood, you're greeted by the sights and smells of one of America's thriving Chinatowns. Streets lined with pagodas and decorative arches beckon you into family-owned restaurants, traditional grocery stores, and souvenir shops. You'll find Mandarin and Cantonese influences alongside Sichuan and Taiwanese in this culturally rich, growing community. Take the Red Line train to Cermak-Chinatown station or board the water taxi in the Loop. Free and metered parking is available.

1

Named for a pillar of the community
There's four tall dragons that line the entry
Stroll the bamboo grove and the ginkgo trees
Catching the water taxi is a breeze.

2

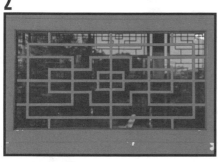

Ready to take a spin on the river?
Well, this bright red structure will surely deliver
Or sit back and relax and watch others row
Under the white canopy—just take it slow.

_____

_____

3

HONOR - DUTY - FAM

華裔退伍

AN LEGIOI

Family, community, and love of nation
For these they fought in foreign locations
These Chinatown neighbors were truly selfless
From all branches we honor their service.

_____

_____

4

A chef nicknamed "Mayor of Chinatown"
Started a trend serving food from Sichuan
Folks line up for the dry chili chicken
It's spicy, numbing, and finger lickin'.

_____

_____

5

Your friends will know this is where you're at
If you say to them, "Meet me at the rat"
Horse, pig, and ox are also in this space
Once a railyard, now a gathering place.

_____

_____

6

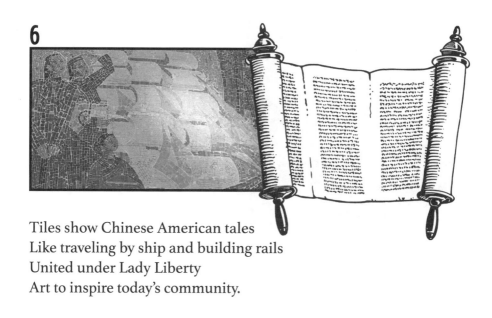

Tiles show Chinese American tales
Like traveling by ship and building rails
United under Lady Liberty
Art to inspire today's community.

7

If you're in the mood for a treat
Try this room full of colorful sweets
Stock up on dried fruit, Yan Yan, and Pocky
And tasty snacks ranging from seaweed to cookies.

8

The best food array and value around
Hidden in a basement, deep underground
Dumplings, stir fry, and boba—find them all
Downstairs beneath this unassuming mall.

9

The prior clue was their first location
Then demand grew for their doughy creations
Try chicken or sea urchin steamed or fried
They're also known by the nickname QXY.

10

A 3D dragon 'neath the Metra tracks
Photos guide you through the neighborhood's acts
Vibrant paintings of past and present cheers
Honor Chinatown's first one hundred years.

_____

_____

11

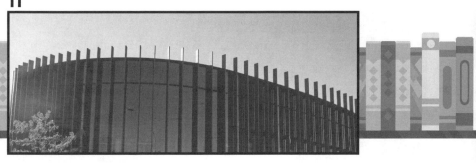

The design concepts of feng shui
Ensure harmony doesn't stray
This curved glass building gets some looks
Filled with Chinese and other books.

_____

_____

12

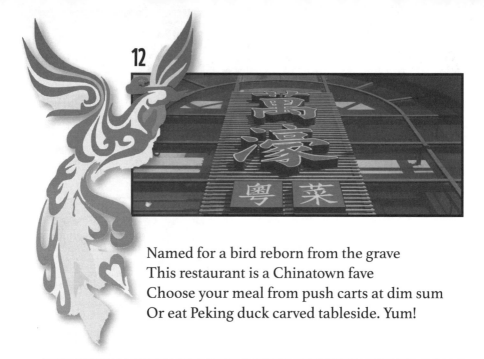

Named for a bird reborn from the grave
This restaurant is a Chinatown fave
Choose your meal from push carts at dim sum
Or eat Peking duck carved tableside. Yum!

13

On Cermak you'll find nine creatures dancing
You'll think you're in Beihai Park Beijing
Vibrant symbols sacred and magical
Look close for five hundred more (they're small!)

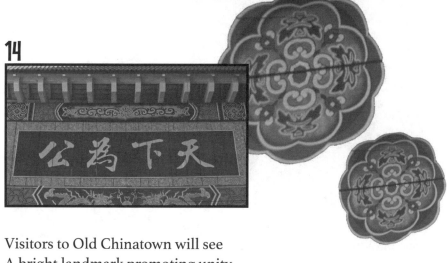

14

Visitors to Old Chinatown will see
A bright landmark promoting unity
In greeting, the Chinese characters spell
"The world belongs to the commonwealth."

15

Red and green pagoda-style towers
Trimmed with terra-cotta lions and flowers
Community center from the On Leong
Now it's a landmark and local icon.

16

Chinatown's oldest bakery
Serves fresh buns sweet and savory
In '86 they got their start
Don't miss the pork buns and egg tarts.

_____

_____

17

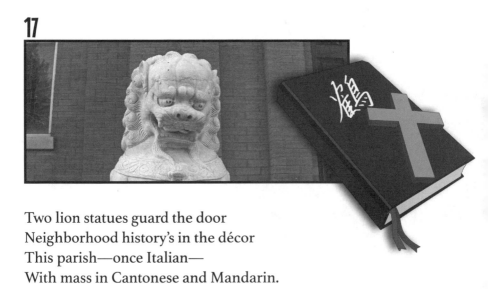

Two lion statues guard the door
Neighborhood history's in the décor
This parish—once Italian—
With mass in Cantonese and Mandarin.

_____

_____

18

Chinese Americans in the Midwest
Featured at this 23rd Street address
Exhibits share culture and history
So important to America's rich story.

19

Chinese chess is still a favorite game
Within this small park with a famous name
President and once revolutionary
His principles included democracy.

Pilsen

Latinx culture thrives in the Lower West Side neighborhood of Pilsen. Since the 1950s, Pilsen has been home to a vibrant, mostly Mexican community. Named for a Czech city by its earlier immigrant residents, you can still spot Central European influences. With colorful street art and fantastic food around every corner, you'll see why Pilsen has attracted emerging artists in recent years. Take the Pink Line to 18th station. Free and metered parking is available.

1

A missionary made his camp nearby
And gave exploring the New World a try
A trail that native people delivered
Connected the Great Lakes and Great River.

2

Built by members of its parish group
Twin spires were taller than buildings in Loop
Featuring common brick on a Gothic scale
The church was even built without a nail!

3

J.A.C.

When you board the train at Damen station
Look out for Angel Chavez's creation
A tree with its roots and local faces
Celebrate Pilsen's neighborhood spaces.

4

While strolling down Cullerton look around
A muralist's home is easily found
Gulliver in barbed wire breaking free
Speaks to immigration and identity.

_____

_____

5

Featuring Mexican art and culture
Collections from both sides of the border
Work by Aztecs and Rivera you'll see
Museum admission is always free.

_____

_____

6

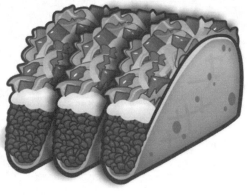

Seek the sign with the white pig if you're a fan
Of the tasty flavors of Michoacan
Juicy pork is slow-cooked—it'll bring you to tears.
And diners have returned for forty years.

_____

_____

7

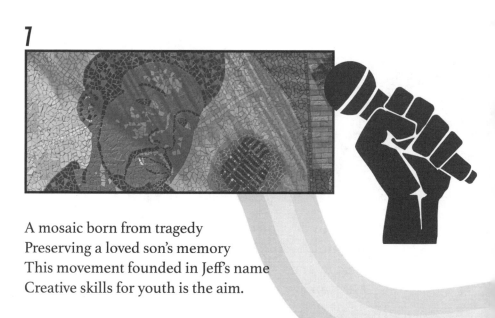

A mosaic born from tragedy
Preserving a loved son's memory
This movement founded in Jeff's name
Creative skills for youth is the aim.

_____

_____

8

A vibrant mural found along 18th
It celebrates queer identities
The artist Sam Kirk represented pride
In her community on the South Side.

9

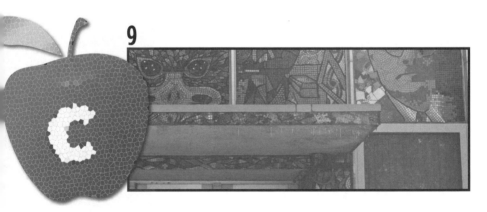

Thousands of tiles glitter like jewels
Mosaics covering the front of this school
Teachers and students worked to represent
Mexican figures most prominent.

10

Behind a high school that bears his name
Historic figures of Mexican fame
Leaders like Zapata and Madero
This President who is still a hero.

_____

_____

11

On Blue Island Ave. you know where to go
To find the perfect, authentic taco
It starts with whole-kernel corn that is ground
Here you'll discover the best bites around.

_____

_____

12

Are you craving a caffeine stop?
Look out for the legume that hops
Order yourself a "screaming bean"
And pause to admire the local art scene.

_____

_____

13

Family-owned for over forty years
They specialize in fried, sugary spears
Chocolate, caramel, or guava treats
And even yummy vegan sweets.

_____

_____

Heading west from the Chicago River
Where inspiring street murals deliver
The neighborhood's culture and history
This embankment's now an outdoor gallery.

15

This building on Allport Street you'll see
Named for the Greek muse of comedy
Greenman watches over the door
Inside are concerts and a dance floor.

16

Like a saloon from the Old West
Head where the barbecue is the best
Their pulled pork is tasty—as everyone knows
Live jazz and blues have you tapping your toes.

17

The mural you see was painted bright
After the first one was covered in white
A butterfly and Aztec deity
Flanked by heroes of the community.

18

Sign with a globe marks this nonprofit's home
Where shelves are lined with donated tomes
Proceeds from discounted books that you buy
Will help their literacy programs thrive.

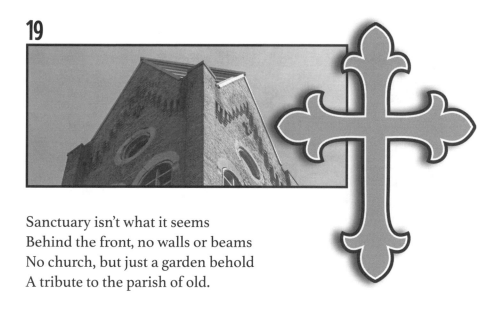

Sanctuary isn't what it seems
Behind the front, no walls or beams
No church, but just a garden behold
A tribute to the parish of old.

Bridgeport

The South Side community area of Bridgeport is home to
bungalows and baseball. Its first residents were Irish immigrants
who labored digging the Illinois and Michigan canal, and other
ethnic groups followed to work in the nearby Union Stock Yard.
Once the center of Chicago's "machine" politics, today Bridgeport
draws supporters of its growing arts scene, innovative restaurants,
and the Chicago White Sox. Take the Red Line to Sox-35th
station. Free street parking is available.

1

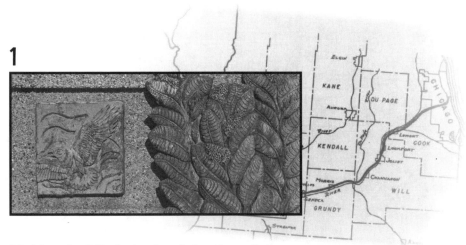

Linking the Mississippi and the Great Lakes
Was a project weighted with massive stakes
Where the I&M Canal used to flow
As it helped a young Chicago to grow.

2

Sreoll down Canalport Riverwalk Park
See thirty-five giants in a skyline stark
Storing so much grain here was a feat
Chicago became the "Stacker of Wheat."

3

Sharp roofs that jut into the sky
Like rowers' oars you see nearby
This public space that delivers
Interaction with the river.

4

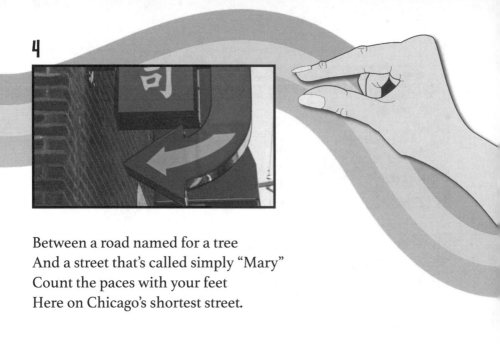

Between a road named for a tree
And a street that's called simply "Mary"
Count the paces with your feet
Here on Chicago's shortest street.

_____

_____

5

This park has quite a backstory
Once a landfill and a quarry
Hike to the top for skyline views
Don't forget your fishing pole, too.

_____

_____

6

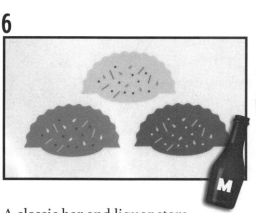

A classic bar and liquor store
The matriarch's name is over the door
If you're hungry, grab nearby seats
And enjoy Korean Polish eats.

7

Outside, bright prayer flags mark the site
Where people go to get enlightened
Once a church, Root's final design
Hosts many Buddhas, found inside.

8

Monks aren't often found in the city
But these Benedictines run a B&B
Gothic details from gargoyle to pew
Their classic Gregorian chant will move you.

9

A circle by another name
Cultural programming is its aim
See an event or an art show
It also hosts local radio.

10

Spiegel showed people what to wear
And also created the teddy bear
These days it's an art and design home
With galleries and studios you can roam.

11

At the previous clue find an anchor
Then head towards the cutely named water
Where gas from a grisly dumping ground
Creates gurgles that can still be found.

12

The city was built where two watersheds meet
This maritime story's vital and offbeat
Aquatic history from fur traders
To canoes and steamships, tugboats and freighters.

_____

_____

13

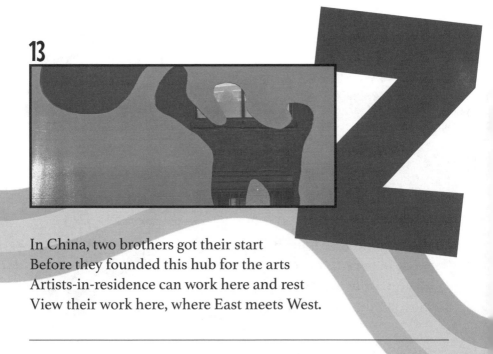

In China, two brothers got their start
Before they founded this hub for the arts
Artists-in-residence can work here and rest
View their work here, where East meets West.

_____

_____

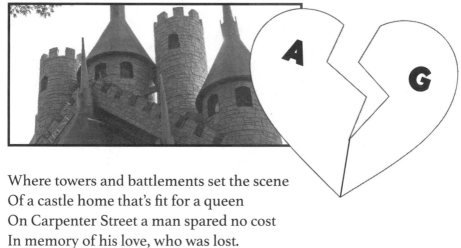

Where towers and battlements set the scene
Of a castle home that's fit for a queen
On Carpenter Street a man spared no cost
In memory of his love, who was lost.

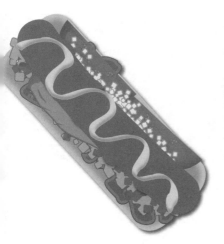

15

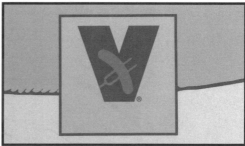

If your lunchtime needs an upgrade
Go to where the sausage is made
Been in the biz since the World's Fair
Chicago dogs are on the menu there.

16

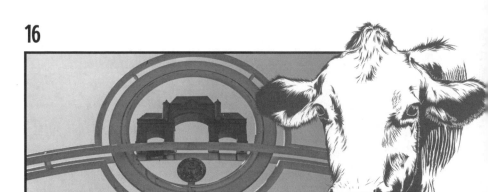

Just a few blocks south in Back of the Yards
Sherman the cow o'er three arches stands guard
Livestock once filled it from front to rear
When the "hog butcher to the world" was here.

17

Come in and stop by for a beer
Four generations have worked here
A tavern near where they play ball
It's nicknamed "little city hall."

18

Bridgeport to five mayors was home
And two of them called this house their own.
The Boss built a home on South Lowe
Go and find his brick bungalow.

19

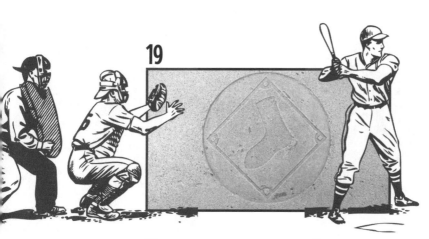

Keep an eye out near gate five
Home plate is all that survives
For 80 years home of the Sox
Today you'll find a parking lot.

Bronzeville

Nicknamed the "Black Metropolis," Bronzeville is the historic center of African American culture and innovation in Chicago. During the early 20th century, thousands of African Americans moved to this area from the South as part of the Great Migration. Walk in the footsteps of icons like Louis Armstrong and Gwendolyn Brooks, and see how the South Side neighborhood continues its rich legacy today. Take the Green Line to 35th-Bronzeville-IIT station. Free and metered street parking is available.

1

Worn shoe soles make up his suit
Case full of dreams in his grip
He's facing north along this route
Where thousands before made this trip.

2

The Little Giant gave his land
To train here under Abe's command
Prisoners of war lived under strain
But now only this plaque remains.

3

In a park of his name, he stands
Holding a book with one raised hand
Got his start with *Oak and Ivy*
"Dream on," his words resound wisely.

4

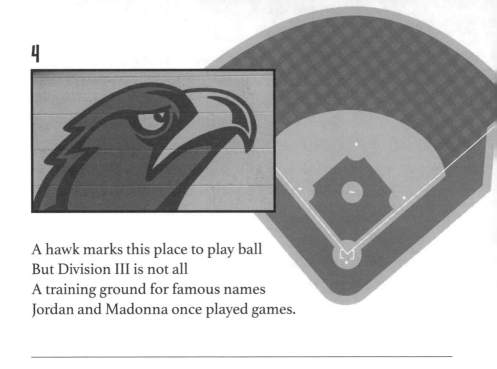

A hawk marks this place to play ball
But Division III is not all
A training ground for famous names
Jordan and Madonna once played games.

_____

_____

5

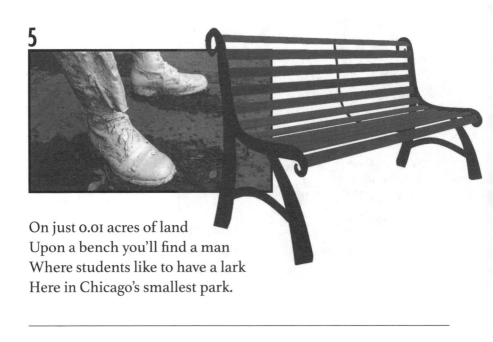

On just 0.01 acres of land
Upon a bench you'll find a man
Where students like to have a lark
Here in Chicago's smallest park.

_____

_____

6

Doing a keg stand or taking a test
Under a tube, faceless figures rest
At a building designed by someone Kool
Portraying the architect of this school.

7

Named for a very fancy hat
Built on the site of Mecca Flats
A floating box of space and scale
Proof that "God is in the details."

8

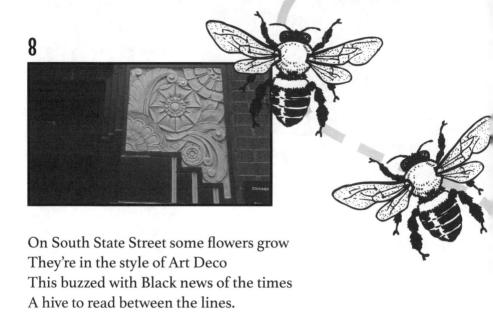

On South State Street some flowers grow
They're in the style of Art Deco
This buzzed with Black news of the times
A hive to read between the lines.

_____

_____

9

Center for African Americans
(No, the Village People didn't appear)
The site of important social actions
Black History Month was born here.

_____

_____

The nation's first museum of Black art
It was created by the WPA
A space that has Black culture at its heart
It's still hosting exhibitions today.

11

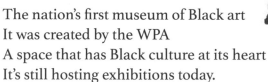

Bronzeville's future, past, and present
Gwendolyn and Harold looking vibrant
Artists and students worked in synergy
To highlight this source of green energy.

12

A shop now sells beauty supplies
But in its past is a surprise
Louis, Cab, and Benny all played
On this stage in its jazz club days.

13

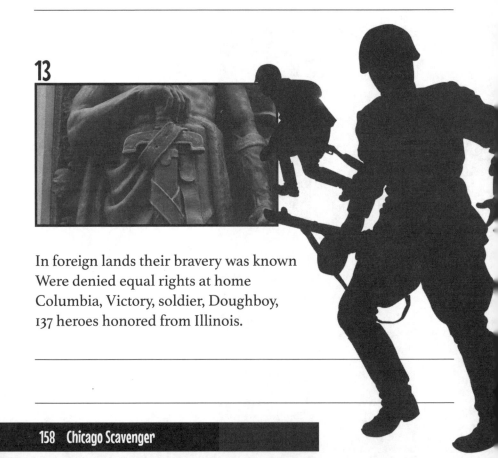

In foreign lands their bravery was known
Were denied equal rights at home
Columbia, Victory, soldier, Doughboy,
137 heroes honored from Illinois.

14

Look down and you'll find the renowned names
Of Black Chicagoans with claims to fame
Sam Cooke and Bessie Coleman pave the way
Welcoming you to Bronzeville today.

<hr />

<hr />

15

Here lived a legendary reporter
Who exposed racism and *Southern Horrors*
She marched for women's rights, not in the back
Integrating suffrage for white and Black.

<hr />

<hr />

16

Nat and Muddy here graced the stage
Concerts and movements packed the hall
The empty brick giant seeks a new age
Commerce and entertainment for all.

17

A new sound born from tragedy
Blending faith with blues melody
The first gospel choir raised its voice
Now, folks around the world rejoice.

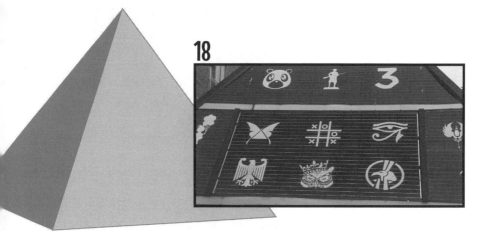

18

When it is dark outside, it still shines
But this structure's not a pharaoh's shrine
The hieroglyphics of modern students
Adorn an energy source most prudent.

19

If it's Southern food you crave
Their shrimp and grits is all the rave
Go take a drive down MLK
And savor breakfast served all day.

Hyde Park

Hyde Park's identity as a cultural hub was sealed after hosting the 1893 World's Fair and the University of Chicago. It's known for innovation, with famous firsts like the Ferris wheel and the nuclear reaction. Hyde Park has always been home to freethinkers appreciating art, science, architecture, and good food. It was even home to a President! Take the Red Line to Garfield station or the Metra to 55th–56th–57th Street station. Free and metered street parking is available.

1

Opened long ago by Greek immigrants
A favorite of Chicago's President
It's the subject of the *Slim's Table* book
From short ribs to omelettes, they can cook!

2

Chocolate cone and one sweet start
Is what sets this corner apart
On 53rd street stands a rock
Where young Michelle first kissed Barack.

3

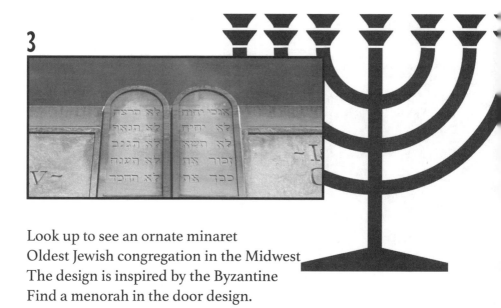

Look up to see an ornate minaret
Oldest Jewish congregation in the Midwest
The design is inspired by the Byzantine
Find a menorah in the door design.

4

There are two fountains that are called the same
On a street that also bears this name
The Southern fountain's the oldest in town
Named for one never on our city ground.

5

Sitting in Washington Park you'll see
The oldest museum of Black history
Covering social justice, culture, and more
With a wing on the city's first Black mayor.

6

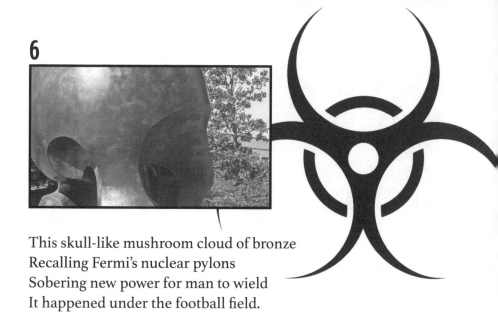

This skull-like mushroom cloud of bronze
Recalling Fermi's nuclear pylons
Sobering new power for man to wield
It happened under the football field.

7

At this passage where dragons stop
Like students climbing to the top
Enter the main quad from the north
Under the architect's name go forth.

8

It was a research lab outdoors
Attracting ducks—and fans—by the score
Turtles and peaceful garden landscapes
Offer a calming nature escape.

_____

_____

9

A mile-long lawn between two parks
Held the Ferris wheel and other larks
A Swedish scientist marks this nook
Where you can sit and enjoy a book.

_____

_____

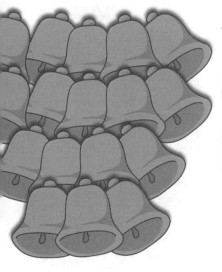

10

Sounds of carillon chimes carry
From this Gothic sanctuary
One hundred faces of stone greet you
Roosevelt, Plato, and Dante, too!

11

Ancient artifacts wait inside
From the Middle East, far and wide
East meets West above the entry
Where it reads, "We behold thy beauty."

12

The Prairie Style is what it defines
Emphasizing horizontal lines
Recalling the landscape of the Midwest
This building is listed among Frank's best.

_____

_____

13

Hyde Park's bookish folks tend to flock
To two shops located 'round the block
One named for students of theology
The other is known for tomes literary.

_____

_____

14

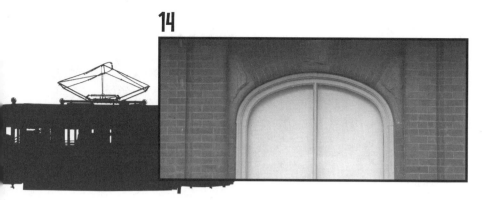

When the World's Fair brought in extra people
This building was a cable car depot
It's now restored to its former glory
And helps to share the neighborhood's story.

15

This scenic spot in Burnham Park is renowned
For stunning views of Hyde Park and downtown
A bronze fawn invites you to stay awhile
At this man-made park in the Prairie Style.

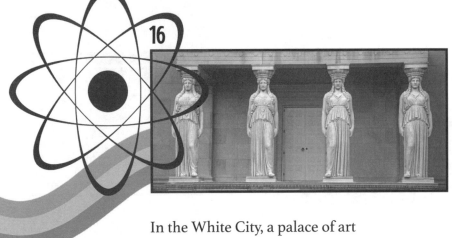

16

In the White City, a palace of art
And now a palace of scientific smarts
Four women stand outside, looking aloof
Their heads are bearing the weight of the roof.

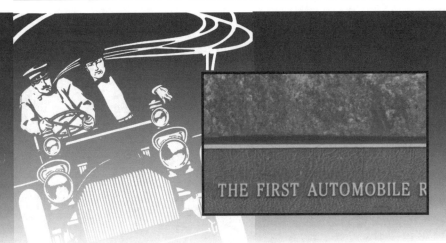

THE FIRST AUTOMOBILE R

Thanksgiving Day in '95
Six cars lined up here to drive
Zooming round-trip to Evanston
Nine hours until the trip was done!

18

Next to a garden gifted from Japan
On the Wooded Island this sculpture stands
You'll see lotus petals reaching up tall
A message of peace and harmony for all.

19

Traffic stops here for this glowing lady
Who holds an eagle and Liberty
Twenty-four-foot tall the shining visual
Mini of the World's Fair original.

Pullman

Chicago is home to the only national monument in Illinois. Pullman was a company town built on utopian ideals in 1881 for employees of the Pullman Palace Car Company. Critical to US labor history, its workers organized both an 1894 strike and the first African American labor union in 1925. As you walk Pullman's picturesque streets, the brick homes built for executives and laborers still tell a fascinating story. Take the Metra to 111th Street station. Free street parking is plentiful.

1

The first museum of Black labor history
Chronicles a 1937 victory
After years of working for meager pay,
Their strike—led by Randolph—is remembered today.

2

When visiting Pullman, here's where you start
This building was at the factory's heart
A giant clock shows where you can enter
For info at the visitor center.

_____

_____

3

Under the Metra viaduct you'll see
An artwork sharing local history
Depicting porters and the President
Naming Pullman a national monument.

_____

_____

4

This stately Queen Anne building's a sight
Where Pullman's distinguished guests spent the night
Its name a tribute to the boss's daughter.
(And you could buy a drink stronger than water!)

_____

_____

5

Stroll around where the gardens grow
Named for a building gone long ago
A bed of roses just to the north
Honors the strike of '94.

_____

_____

6

A treasured historic exhibit hall
Canvas for this gorgeous mural
Created by talented students of art
Portraying workers and a train car.

7

Near arches find a horse's head
For they made this building their bed
This was the whole town's livery
Helping to keep Pullman's streets tidy.

8

Next door to the previous clue
Who could afford a park-side view?
Officials and the like could pay
They still make lovely homes today.

_____

_____

9

Look up at the lofty, pointed steeple
Built for the worship of all the townspeople
Still central to the neighborhood today
The material's name gives it away.

_____

_____

10

This boardinghouse once became medical
For years it served as the town's hospital
If it's familiar, you could relive
The one-armed man's story from *The Fugitive*.

11

When you see arches all around
These curved, two-story flats you've found
In the center all that remains
Once used for meat, veggies, and grains.

12

The largest houses in town you'll see
Were home to bigwigs by the factory
Admire this fine home of an immigrant
Who worked his way up to superintendent.

13

Where two historic brick buildings
Are now affordable housing
Here, artists can live and create
Their shared gallery space is great.

14

Known elsewhere as tenements
Block houses were Pullman's cheapest rents
Named for a relative of the founder
Now the office of an historic center.

15

Find this brick building to hit the books
Use the right entrance or you'll get looks
And right behind it on Forrestville
Pay tribute at the war memorial.

16

As you walk along Champlain Ave
Look for buildings with front doors three
Four flats here for young couples to have
With cheap rents for the just married.

17

Take a quick drive to Roseland and see Mr. B
He's made sweets for half a century
Line up early for his apple fritters
Treats iced in chocolate or glazed in sugar.

18

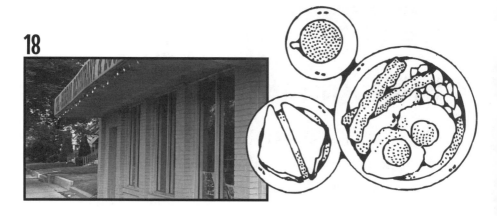

If you want some breakfast look no farther
Than this diner named for a body of water
More than forty years this dining room
Has been the neighborhood's best greasy spoon.

19

If you're hungry I know a place
With three restaurants in one space
Where entrepreneurs hit their stride
Come get a taste of the South Side.

Bibliography

I encourage using resources to help the seeker find the way and have included a list of works that I found helpful in crafting *Chicago Scavenger*.

39th Annual Pullman House Tour, Historic Pullman Foundation, Chicago, IL, 2012.

Adelman, William J. Touring Pullman: *A Study in Company Paternalism: A Walking Guide to the Pullman Community in Chicago, Illinois*. Illinois Labor History Society, 1977.

Bizzarri, Amy. *Discovering Vintage Chicago: A Guide to the City's Timeless Shops, Bars, Delis & More*. Globe Pequot, 2015.

Block Club Chicago, Block Club Chicago, https://blockclubchicago.org/.

Borzo, Greg. *Chicago's Fabulous Fountains*. Southern Illinois University Press, 2017.

Butler, Patrick. *Hidden History of Lincoln Park*. History Press, 2015.

Chicago Architecture Center, Chicago Architecture Center, https://www.architecture.org/.

Chicago Chinatown Chamber of Commerce, Chicago Chinatown Chamber of Commerce, https://www.chicagochinatown.org/chinatown-landmark.

Chicago Landmarks, City of Chicago, https://webapps1.chicago.gov/landmarksweb.

Chicago Magazine, Chicago Magazine, https://www.chicagomag.com/.

Chicago Park District | The Official Website of the Chicago Park District, Chicago Park District, https://www.chicagoparkdistrict.com/.

The Chicago Public Art Guide, City of Chicago, https://www.chicago.gov/content/dam/city/depts/dca/Public%20Art/publicartguide1.pdf.

Chicago Sun-Times, Chicago Sun-Times, https://chicago.suntimes.com/.

Chicago Tribune, Tribune Publishing, https://www.chicagotribune.com/.

Chicago, IL Patch, Patch Media, https://patch.com/illinois/chicago.

Choose Chicago, Choose Chicago, https://www.choosechicago.com/.

Cohn, Scotti. *Chicago Curiosities: Quirky Characters, Roadside Oddities, & Other Offbeat Stuff*. Globe Pequot Press, 2010.

CTA, Chicago Transit Authority , https://www.transitchicago.com/.

Enjoy Illinois, Illinois Department of Commerce & Economic Opportunity, https://www.enjoyillinois.com/.

Ford, Anne. *Peaceful Places Chicago: 119 Tranquil Sites in the Windy City and Beyond*. Menasha Ridge Press, 2011.

Forgotten Chicago, Forgotten Chicago, https://forgottenchicago.com/.

Gray, Mary Lackritz. *A Guide to Chicago's Murals*. University of Chicago Press, 2001.

Grossman, James R. Edited by Janice L Reiff and Ann Durkin Keating, *Encyclopedia of Chicago*, Chicago History Museum, The Newberry Library, and Northwestern University, http://encyclopedia.chicagohistory.org/.

Holden, Greg. *Literary Chicago: A Book Lover's Tour of the Windy City*. Lake Claremont Press, 2001.

Koenig, Wendy, and Christine Badowski. Chicago Public Art, http://chicagopublicart.blogspot.com/.

Landscape Architect, Landscape Communications Inc., https://landscapearchitect.com/.

Lane, George, and Algimantas Kezys. *Chicago Churches and Synagogues: An Architectural Pilgrimage*. Loyola University Press, 1981.

Loerzel, Robert. *Walking Chicago: 35 Tours of the Windy City's Dynamic Neighborhoods and Famous Lakeshore*. Wilderness Press, 2020.

Medill Reports Chicago, Northwestern University, https://news.medill.northwestern.edu/chicago/.

Mlinaric, Jessica. *Secret Chicago: A Guide to the Weird, Wonderful, and Obscure*. Reedy Press, 2018.

National Parks Service, U.S. Department of the Interior, https://www.nps.gov.

National Trust for Historic Preservation, National Trust for Historic Preservation, https://savingplaces.org/.

News, Views and the Energy Future, Commonwealth Edison Company, https://www.comed.com/News/Pages/Default.aspx.

Open House Chicago, Chicago Architecture Center , https://openhousechicago.org/.

Sinkevitch, Alice, and Laurie McGovern Petersen. *AIA Guide to Chicago*. University of Illinois Press, 2014.

South Side Weekly, South Side Weekly, https://southsideweekly.com/best-chinatown-2017/.

Srivastava, Jyoti. Public Art in Chicago, http://chicago-outdoor-sculptures.blogspot.com/.

Street Art News, Street Art News, https://streetartnews.net/.

Studio Gang, Studio Gang, https://studiogang.com.

Time Out Chicago, Time Out, https://www.timeout.com/chicago.

Tubens, Luis. "Virtual Tour | Pilsen Murals Walking Tour." 8 June 2021, Chicago, IL, Chicago History Museum.

Uptown United, Uptown United & The Uptown Chamber of Commerce, https://exploreuptown.org/.

WBEZ Chicago, Chicago Public Media, https://www.wbez.org/.

Witter, David Anthony. *Oldest Chicago, Second Edition*. Reedy Press, 2020.

WTTW, WTTW, https://www.wttw.com/.

Zangs, Mary. *The Chicago 77: A Community Area Handbook*. The History Press, 2014.